BUILDING TO LAST

ARCHITECTURE AS ONGOING ART

by HERB GREENE

with Nanine Hilliard Greene

ARCHITECTURAL BOOK PUBLISHING COMPANY

New York 10016

Also by Herb Greene

MIND AND IMAGE
University Press of Kentucky, Lexington 1976
Granada Publishing Ltd., London 1980

Library of Congress Cataloging in Publication Data

Greene, Herb.   Building to last.

  Includes index.
  1. Architecture.   2. Building—Remodeling for other
use.   3. Architecture—Decision-making.   4. Group
work in architecture.   I. Greene, Nanine Hilliard,
joint author.   II. Title.
NA2500.G677   720   80-39548
ISBN 0-8038-0028-2

Published simultaneously in Canada by
Saunders of Toronto, Ltd., Don Mills, Ontario

Designed by Al Lichtenberg

Printed in the United States of America

Contents

ACKNOWLEDGEMENTS

We wish to express our appreciation to everyone who
participated in the preparation of this book: to The
National Endowment for the Arts for a research grant;
to Jim Burns and Jim Morgan, AIA, for reading and editorial
suggestions; George Collins for obtaining illustrations;
Max Hall for inspiration for the title; Susan Bower for
the concept of the health center; Rob Donaldson for the
concept of the urban stage set; Mike Schmidt for help with
the neighborhood armature and the armature for public
services; Lynne Funk for research and proofreading; Jeff
Wagner and Dennis Carpenter for photoprinting; Barbara T.
Coleman for typing; and to the many others whose names
appear on illustrations and in the notes.

Herb Greene
and Nanine Hilliard Greene

Preface

PREVAILING economic and technological forces and aesthetic attitudes have tended, in cities around the world, to level the historic artifice, leaving in its place new buildings with disorienting and anonymous form. In these discussions I want to offer a strategy whereby history and place are again built into the city. I address the question of how we can create new buildings that not only enhance the sense of place but are likely to get better as they get older. To conserve resources we need a process that produces a building type that is solid and long-lasting, yet responsive to additions, alterations and ornamentation by individuals over generations and that can become a record of their aesthetic and social commentary. In the western world today, renewed growth of the arts and crafts among citizens, the widening interest in art in the public environment, the currency of collage as an art form, and the aesthetic, social, and energy conserving possibilities of labor-intensive building methods represent changes in climate that encourage me to make these proposals. In spite of the fragmentation of interest groups and ethnic diversity, I believe most people long for symbols in which they can share identity and for work in which their self-expression lives after them.

I have been most moved by architecture that shows the efforts of many people bound together by common purpose to create a transcendent aesthetic form. Contrary to the mainstream in Modern architecture I have never accepted the machine as a model for either functional or aesthetic form but have continued to believe that human spontaneity, cultural continuity and an organic connection to nature are primary sources in creating architecture of the deepest and most lasting appeal. I have also wondered how the architect can, in a specific building, express its historic origins, evolution and multiple meanings.

The more I try to hypothesize how on-going structures, which I call armatures, can actually be built, the more I realize the difficulties that tax the credibility of the theory. However, most strategies prerequisite to armatures already exist: preservation laws protect buildings, neighborhoods and districts in many cities; retirees and skilled craftspersons work for nominal wages or as volunteers in VISTA and the Peace Corps. A town in Denmark puts unemployed teenagers to work building boxes for the local fishing industry at wage rates set by the community. Crafts groups making handmade bricks for an armature may find, like the Danish youths building boxes, that there is an expanding profitable market for their products. We already have models of complex decision-making in public-private ventures underway in many cities. We need only to restructure these procedures in order to build armatures.

As the reader becomes acquainted with the book, I hope the armature can be seen as a generic idea that can be approached from many directions. Although I have made drawings suggesting the architecture of armatures and have included related examples as begun by a few others, this is not a how-to book. I am more concerned with *what* to do and *why* to do it. My drawings are suggestions to help visualize an idea and not final plans for ready-to-build architecture. Even if accepted as images that do not claim to be architecture, the formal preferences of one architect cannot please everyone but should at least stimulate alternatives.

Architecture inevitably calls for a wholistic approach. I have tried to be aware of the economic, political and social implications that others in those fields can deal with in more depth. Necessarily, I must write from the standpoint of architecture, art and design since that is my experience. If anything is to be changed in the present commercial building milieu with its lack of creative craftsmanship and declining urban quality, many people with appropriate expertise will have to move together. This book strives to give a vision of tangible objectives and common desires in the belief that if the hypothesis has vitality, it may stimulate others toward sharper focus and possible realizations.

Part One / PUBLIC CONTEXT

1 An Armature Way of Building

I am standing in the city square. Around me is paving laid with a multitude of inscriptions and designs. Like an enormous tapestry, a colorful wave, it sweeps up the sides of the surrounding three-story buildings where roofs reveal gardens, canopies, banners and glassy skylights. Towering behind and above are offices, hotels and apartments gridded in steel and concrete. But it is the base structures that hold me. Nearby they resemble not so much a building as a kind of banded and eroded cliff vaguely reminiscent of the stratified limestone formations along a nearby river, while further off at the end of the block they transform into shapes that resemble buildings.

Breaking into these streaming bands, I see an image of Victorian mansard with Italianate windows, remnants of the first City Hall destroyed many years ago. There is a warmth of color in this earthy background made lustrous with glazed pottery and mottled with deep shadowy reliefs. One wall graduates from red-browns to purples, the shades of local clays predominating in the bricks of older buildings in the city. Texture is pervasive. Shadows, niches, unfinished areas and reliefs in human scale let me merge with the wall. As I follow one passage in the collage of ornament, impressions taken from nearby fossil beds transform into the works of eight-year-olds, their photos and hand prints re-cessed into finger-painted ceramic blocks. At street level, extending into the square, are colorful awnings and additions—outdoor restaurants, flowers in portable tubs, an entrance to a hotel, sidewalk sales, kiosks and shop windows. Looking back across the plaza to the encrusted wall I see discs of magenta, azure blue and pearl placed near what appear to be black apertures. These floating circles look like planets in a medium full of mysterious inflections. There is a dreamlike aspect to the image. Shifts in outline, allusions to various examples of historic architecture and the emergence of surprising images support the dream. Yet the thick-walled and solid structures project substance and age. They seem to have always been here.

IN this book an armature is a public element in a neighborhood or city core to which space-enclosing structures and ornamental surfaces of individual determination can be added or subtracted. It is solid and long lasting. It is richly encrusted with the crafts and arts of as many as thousands of participating citizens. Since buildings constitute a principal part of production and are a basic necessity, an armature provides on-going work and an outlet for the talents of citizens not now included in the building process. The accretion of people's art

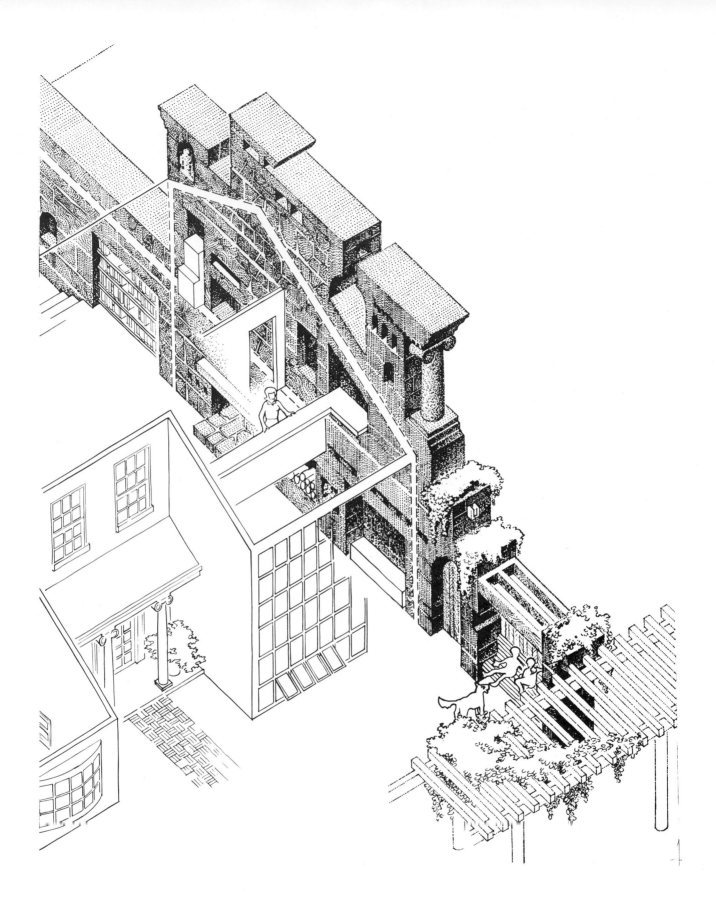

Neighborhood armature with private housing attached (detail). Residents can add and subtract from a long-lasting solid structure that provides niches, hearths and habitable space within itself. The concept of an armature can include common open spaces, community gardens, public paving, and walls controlled and ornamented by citizens. (*Drawing by Herb Greene.*)

and craft work and the modification of certain spaces and forms designed by architects to accommodate alterations, make the structure a vehicle of cultural memory, a medium for expressing change and a metaphor for the passage of time.

The concept of an armature is not, of course, completely new. A few contemporary architects have designed structural and utilitarian frameworks which can be added to by users. Many examples of folk building show satisfactory and even beautiful building stock which has evolved over the course of time. One role of an armature is the recovery of the malleability and human scale of this preindustrial vernacular.

While much world architecture has expressed the historic continuum with rich and memorable forms, the armature, in addition, will foster an aesthetic egalitarianism not found in either past or present architecture, but which is necessary as an expression of democratic and pluralist societies. Democratic expression in armatures is not limited to aesthetics. An important distinction between the armature way of building and a megastructure approach to the design of cities is that armatures embody guidelines to produce a public form of architecture amenable to community participation and group consensus in determining and perpetuating the long-lasting framework. While an armature can become a large-scaled container of architectural space which organizes and houses a variety of functions, it can also be as small as the service gatehouse of a residential neighborhood. It can incorporate and preserve a block of scattered historically-valued buildings; it can be a comprehensible form designed to identify an important urban space; and finally it can be the principal organizer of a district or town. In each case it must invite modification and the accretion of citizens' works.

While a megastructure is generally designed as all-of-a-piece by one architect, it is expected that more than one architect will design or add to an armature. It is open to collaborations and requires additions to its frame as well as its surfaces and spaces. An armature, being designed to be added to, will have financial support from numerous sources as it opens itself to additions by smaller users and grass-root involvement by

local people. Unlike a megastructure which often suggests control and financing by big institutions and usually interrupts the fabric of the city or town, an armature with its generally smaller scale, regional references and user additions is intended to respect its surroundings. Although an armature can be a formal element in organizing urban design, I am not proposing it as a planning panacea to solve the functional problems of the city but as a new building strategy to enrich architecture and foster a public loyalty toward buildings that is lacking in modern society. There are four components to an armature program:

1. The basic publicly controlled long-lived poetic framework is designed by architects to be reused indefinitely, built of materials chosen for durability, aesthetic appropriateness, and to conserve resources. As an historic landmark the armature requires the knowledge of historians and preservationists as well as architects. As a vehicle for culture the armature can be a backdrop for art fairs, concerts, dance and theater. Some armatures will also become a focus of tourist interest with attendant revenues.

2. Crafts and arts are continually added by citizens until the armature gradually becomes a diverse, rich record of the community. Work may be carried on at the site or in workshop programs in neighborhood centers, schools and other institutions and by individuals working at home. Craft production will enlist paid and volunteer artists, designers, facilitators, managers, builders and suppliers. As the surfaces and spaces become filled, room must be made for future additions. Pieces of ornament and architectural elements will be recycled in a new armature or sold as decorative pieces.

3. Spaces within the basic framework can be leased for use as shops, housing, offices, public services, or whatever is compatible with the site and context of a particular armature.

4. Additions by private investment can be either small or large depending on the purpose of the armature and whether it is in a neighborhood or city center.

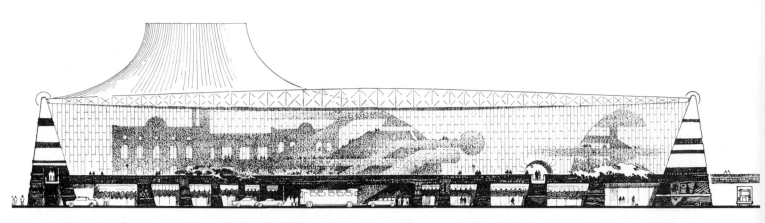

Elevation of an armature for an exhibition building or civic center on a rectangular urban block. The dark structure at the base, faced with people's art, contains shops that front on the interior as well as on the street. The building incorporates three technologies: handcraft on pavings and facades, intermediate technology for alterations to the interior core, and high technology for the contemporary translucent roof membrane and glass walls supported by trusses. The remnants of historic structures incorporated in the interior, like dimly seen ruins, are intended to recall the city's past history and architecture. (*Drawing by Herb Greene.*)

A town creek as the basis for an armature. Additions can be made to the masonry walls of abandoned structures while saving their aesthetically valued forms and textures. Encrustations of citizens' craft and art can give new meaning and establish a more powerful sense of a public realm. The development of the San Antonio River in the heart of the city and more recent projects that are rehabilitating urban water courses show the potential of newly cleaned-up streams, and the usefulness of turning the backs of commercial buildings into fronts. (*Drawing by Herb Greene.*)

12

Armature as urban stage set. Elevation. This armature, replacing a parking lot in the heart of Lexington, Kentucky, evokes images of a grist mill, the earliest type of substantial structure found along nearby rivers. Permanent walls, corners and fragments that allow indeterminate user infill are placed so that interiors and exteriors can be seen in cubist simultaneity. Made of concrete masonry with artists' and citizens' designs formed into terra cotta facings, the walls include a double scale mill corner and an image of rolling wooded hills as backdrop to the outdoor market and screen for day-care facility on second level. Office workers from the surrounding high-rise buildings are likely to shop and lunch at the stalls and boutiques, and bring their children to the day-care center, which will also encourage suburban parents to shop downtown. (*Drawing by Herb Greene.*)

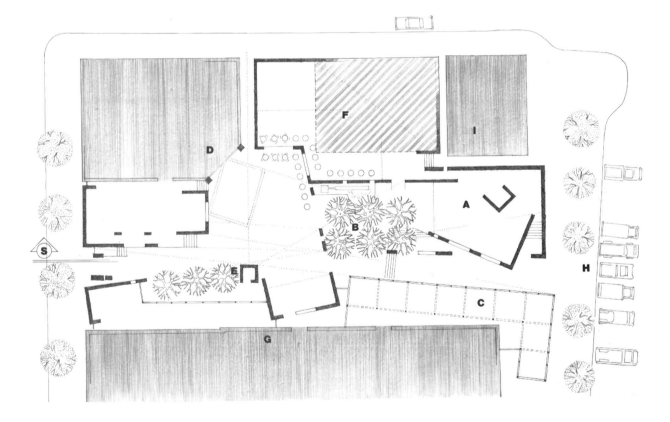

Armature as urban stage set. Plan. (A) User infilled space. (B) Craft or flea market. (C) Winterized market stalls. (D) An existing building that housed a theater in the nineteenth century. One corner is developed as a permanent stage to the outdoor room of the armature. (E) Clock tower. (F) Nondescript one-story building in disrepair is removed to make space for a new restaurant on the ground floor, with a day-care and craft facility for children on the second floor. (G) Three-story brick building is retained. (H) Farmers market currently located on a wide sidewalk fronting a six-lane one-way street. Local farmers back their trucks directly to the curb. (I) Two-story "Georgian" office building built in 1976 is retained. (S with arrow) The elevation is viewed in this direction. (*Drawing by Herb Greene.*)

Armatures are an opportunity to make a synthesis of three technologies: our present high technology, an intermediate technology suited to small groups of citizen-builders, and the return of handcraft. The goal is to bring into the building system thousands of people whose talents are now excluded. This will require combinations of varied technologies and consequently a new aesthetic of diversity and richness. I believe these aims can be realized through gradual adaptations of our present systems of financing, building and design because armatures imply a two-part distinction between the larger-scale public framework which may employ automated technology and big machinery and the small-scale private expressions which are likely to employ intermediate technology and crafts. A building's foundation, structure and utilities can be built with big technology while intermediate-size machines can be appropriate for small additions. I do not see constructing the basic frame by labor-intensive methods unless a group of people choose to build it that way. Individualized craftsmanship can be used principally on walls, paving and decorative parts of the building.

As a building type that maintains its identity over centuries an armature will foster psycho-

A wealth of people's expressions can be made into ornament for architecture. Ingenuous attitudes and direct feeling add qualities that have been all but lost to public architecture. A collage coordination of people's craft and art by facilitators who are artists or architects will result in powerful emotional content as well as humorous juxtapositions. Top: *Photo by Laurence Cuneo.* Bottom: *Photo by Nanine Hilliard Greene.*

logical attachment. Unlike many modern buildings whose images celebrate assembly line production and machines, the first things that come to mind in an armature are visible images of diversity as evidence of democratic action and the power and variety of the human imagination. Also immediate are references to age and to the historic process of accretion. According to Wylie Sypher, all history is dreamlike simply because it is not present. Historical reflection can only sustain and rectify the dream. An armature is a visible dream—an artful image linking the imagined past with immediate action. It is a work of art made by the public fostering a dialogue between past and present with space left open for future voices. It is a continuum rather than a style fixed or isolated in a specific time.

We have begun to acutely miss historic continuity, a sense of place, the gradual improvement of urban spaces by trial and error, and the resonant contrasts gained by more or less harmonious juxtapositions of architecture from different eras. As an element of urban design the armature allows us to recover qualities we have enjoyed in history-filled cities up through the 19th century and in individual buildings which have undergone modifications through generations. Almost all cities in the technologically developed world, subject to the same economic forces and similar attitudes toward design and the use of technology, have lost the ability to continue historic urban quality. Even countries like England and France, in which the

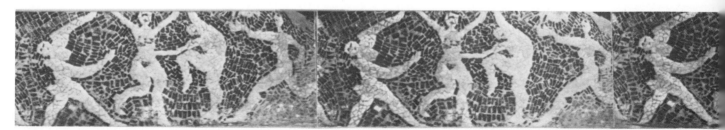

care of the landscape and a wealth of pre-twentieth century buildings often supply the values of beauty and venerability, have experienced the same difficulties designing new towns and new urban developments.

I see an armature way of building as a strategy to recover historic continuity and as an extension to the meaning of organic design. Adaption to specific sites, ethical use and aesthetic expression of materials, poetic expression of function and response to the psychological requirements of users are all criteria for organic architecture. In addition, the armature extends the concept of function to recording a community's existence in time. Ornament, which in the organic tradition always related to a building's purpose and context, on the armature becomes evidence of people's reaction to their place in the historic continuum.

At present architects are seeking a new "Style." The recent International Modern, no matter how noble its original intentions, has made itself finite and self-enclosed. It has become an aesthetic often impervious to adaptation. The most publicized quest today for a subsequent style is being labeled, for lack of an identity of its own, "Post Modern" and appears to be a search for a new visual aesthetic largely based on mannerist manipulations of the Modern and a pastiche with fragments of historic styles. Even at the beginning of the 1980's we have barely begun to expect a building's appearance to reveal a need as urgent as the conservation of energy and natural resources. Nor do our new buildings display an aesthetic resulting from modification by users. In the search for a new "style," architecture has not even addressed itself, as armatures intend to do, to the principle that the talents of the citizen craftsperson and artist have a right to be incorporated into a formal expression of the historic continuum. It is with the realization of a new social philosophy and the necessity of a conservation ethic, that the aesthetics of an armature will evolve.

In an architecture-of-continuum, I am suggesting a way of designing and building that is not a short lived "style." An armature is neither a literal resurrection from the past nor a projection into a science-fiction future. It is the built form of a process continually happening in the present. An armature can transform and incorporate elements from past architecture if these have meaning for local people. An armature can accept current styles or even futuristic additions if desired but the basic framework is always in the present because it is always being built. The process becomes an architecture-of-continuum, a "style" that is never out-of-style because it does not exclude other styles but reincarnates and transforms them within a long-lasting, encompassing form.

Historically, the cultural continuum (sheltered by a relative slow evolutionary process) gave meaning to certain public forms. Now it is widely held that the continuum, broken by rapid technological change and by the end of cultural homogeneity, is never to be repaired.

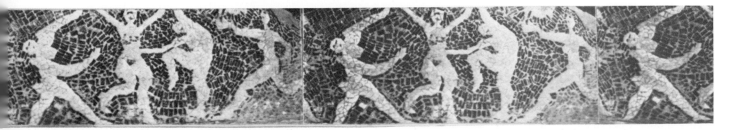

An urban square as an armature. Individual pieces of citizen's art and craft work become a tapestry that flows from pavement to building. Here, colors and detail form a powerful collage that unifies diverse architectural elements.

Armatures suggest a division between the more public, ceremonial and communal uses of a building, and its specific economic and private uses. For instance, buildings surrounding an important urban square in a city may be treated as an armature for the first three floors. To this height ornament shows to best advantage from the square and users' additions and determinations create a genuine public domain. Air rights above three floors can be given over to private development. The armatures may include leased space for the private sector and provide entrances and other required spaces for air rights structures. (*Drawing by Herb Greene.*)

To revitalize commercial cores, many cities are recovering downtown streets for pedestrian use. Washington Street in Boston has new brick paving and protecting canopies as unifying features. The armature concept suggests that a tapestry of citizen designs for similar streets will add crafts-manship, art, and individuality. Infilling vacant sites or renovating buildings as extensions of the street can provide space for public activities beyond the usual commercial life, so that an existing street can gradually be transformed into an armature. (*Photo by Nanine Hilliard Greene.*)

16

An urban armature with cues of ruins. Armatures intend a degree of incompletion combined with symbols of age. Several of my designs suggest ruins. Cues of ruins establish an architecture's dependence on contexts of time past, and imply an original state in which physical and cultural order prevailed; at the same time we see apparent dissolution. We are piqued by this ambivalence and wonder where it came from and how to close the gaps. Thus, ruins allow us to invest the structure with imaginative projections that are not possible in a completed building. (*Drawing by Herb Greene.*)

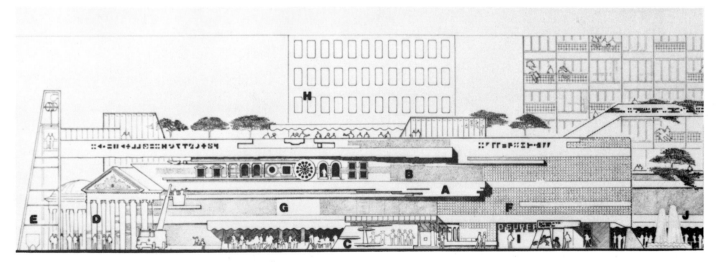

This working drawing of an armature shows a three-story base with a roof garden. The long-lived frame, designed by architects, is intended to be filled in with citizens' art in other generations. The design metaphors, proportions and materials of the frame must have enough character to hold the public interest as surfaces and additions are gradually developed. A private office (H) uses air rights and courtyard access. A lift (E) carries people from the street level to the roof. In some places historic pieces (D) have been reconstituted into the frame. (B) is a space given over to citizen's reliefs and ornament while (G) indicates unfinished spaces left for future infill. A sidewalk pylon (C) invites temporary chalk drawings. (A) is part of the frame designed by architect. (F) is infill of translucent glass blocks. (*Drawing by Herb Greene.*)

17

Armatures reestablish a symbol of cultural continuum. Since the inception of the Modern movement some architects have rejected the need for symbol in architecture, believing today's society has outgrown the need to attach significance to highly symbolic forms. This does not mean, however, that symbols, intentional or unintentional, haven't been a prominent feature of contemporary architecture. Buildings always reveal some aspect of a society's public or private life. Architecture is symbolic, whether we intend it or not, but instead of symbols of power or of taste-making elites, I believe we need to seek symbols of a community of citizen craftspersons and artists and of cues that harmonize our deepest common experience. Our contemporary aesthetic sensibility shows that canons of high art or fine art and people art or folk art are not mutually exclusive. If we can set up the armature process and solve the challenge of designing an architectural continuum that can subsume a diversity of individual symbols, we will, I believe, find that new public form has flowered—a rich, changing collage, symbolic of our world. An armature way of building can revitalize values believed lost to technological change and in so doing foster new values.

Recently programs for people's craft and art have burgeoned. There is evidence of widespread talent and interest. New and traditional art is enjoyed or is at least consumed by a vast new audience. Art education has trained more students than we can find jobs for. Ethnic groups are recapturing their cultural history in the arts, in clothes and by research into family and historic ties. In the U.S. the admiration and preservation of historic architecture has finally become a national *cause célèbre*.

In our society we have never experienced the full impact of an accumulation of people's arts that is dense, rich, and large-scale. It is my conjecture that this accumulation will be a new art symbol in itself and will touch off in a large number of participants an appreciation and involvement not available in current museum programs nor through the media. As an armature is continually contributed to, it will evolve into an historic anthem.

Where industrialization overwhelms us with objects and lessens their value by mass replications and constant replacement, the armature is an object of continuity and permanence and a receptacle for the unique and individual. In contrast to the rewards of status by the acquisition of manufactured objects, the rewards of the armature are the satisfactions of doing and making, the bond of participation in the historic continuum and public recognition of the individuality of each crafted object.

2 The Architect's Role

I have walked in the pastures surrounding this city, across green rolling fields, along white fences and beside black tobacco barns. I know the smell of honeysuckle in summer and the cold gray days of February. I know this city when its maples and oaks are electric yellow and red. I've felt the heavy heat of August and dragged through morning oppressions when snow turns to slush and to ice again. I recognize the people here—stout farmers in pickup trucks, fashionable women from the horse set, blacks who gather at the corner of Smith and Willie, students in bluejeans crossing Limestone Street at noon. Around me the past is present in historic brick and stone, and geologic time is visible in road cuts and at every bend of river and stream. Yet, as Kentucky poet Wendell Berry writes, I must learn more:

"No place is to be learned like a textbook or a course in school, and then turned away from forever on the assumption that one's knowledge of it is complete. What is to be known about it is without limit, and it is endlessly changing. Knowing it is therefore like breathing: it can happen, it stays real, only on the condition that it continues *to happen. As soon as it is recognized that a river— or, for that matter, a home—is not a place but a process, not a fact but an event, there ought to come an immense relief: one can step into the same*

river twice, one can go home again." This morning I meet with truck farmers, citizens and people from city hall to discuss an armature as a shelter for the new Farmers' Market. I must evoke their dreams. Each will have memories and hopes fashioned from experience. I must listen and catch themes weaving their lives with mine and conjure a frame that will unite us in common aspirations. Out of this stream of knowledge and half-spoken visions, I will make an image.

AN armature, in its earliest form, must possess a potent aesthetic. Since it may take generations, even centuries, to bring its additions and surfaces to full development, its basic forms and proportions will have to excite interest and curiosity. To achieve this level of response, an armature requires its architects to be poets. To paraphrase the Book of Job, when the line is stretched and the foundations fastened, the architect will listen for the morning stars as they sing together. Architects will possess what Louis Sullivan praised as the greatest of human powers, sympathy, which includes the capacity to be open to the laughter and tears, the everyday joys, strivings and tribulations that are universal.

The architect will at the same time find ways

to coordinate the work of citizens whose small decisions, small investments, additions and art accumulate to build an architecture of collage. If the diverse abilities of poet and coordinator don't reside in one person, and often they may not, then partnerships of architects, facilitators, artists and engineers will have to come about where each complements the other. Out of this understanding will come ways of working with the community and new forms that resonate with the aspirations of citizens. It is apparent that the architect will have to be far more than philosopher meditating on theoretic possibilities. He or she will also break out of habitual office work patterns and try to learn how citizen-clients use architecture and how they feel about their environment.

To do this the architect will take advantage of new decision making methodologies that include the citizen-user. Today design firms and communities employ a variety of methods to discover what citizens believe to be their desirable futures. "Town Hall" meetings, surveys, interviews, planning and design games, "Take Part" workshops and many other methods which employ an understanding of the dynamics of groups are being practiced by experts in the field of human relationships both to describe problems and to determine solutions. The architect-coordinator will use this new expertise that fosters ongoing understanding between designers and citizens. The Cincinnati firm of Kenneth Cunningham, landscape architects, describes the methodology they use as follows: "We have developed a client decision making process that takes into account the diversity and sometimes conflict within the client group. The process also deals with possible conflict between the client group and external groups and organizations the client wants or needs to pay attention to. The process is also based on increased client and designer awareness. This means everyone will become directly familiar with the site by visiting it in different seasons, developing an appreciation of its physical aspects as well as the economic and other practical roots of the situation. Using this understanding, clients are encouraged to apply their new awareness to creative solutions. Besides providing solutions that best meet their needs, the process generates an environment well accepted and maintained by the client group. In the end, the design team shifts the sense of solution ownership to the clients while maintaining ownership of the process, a condition that creates a sense of pride and willingness on the part of the client group to adapt when problems do arise."

These approaches, which invite many to participate, represent steps toward regaining a public life. The confrontations in urban society, caused by conflicting demands on the same piece of land or uses of a building by heterogeneous groups, require the architect to seek social frameworks for these encounters. Groups can come into being, even though temporary, which are neither the nineteenth century class-stratified image of the public nor the overly individualized image of recent times. These new groupings will be representative of a cross section of a diverse and complex society based on people's desire to take part in environmental decisions as interested citizens rather than as guardians of property and social status. As a society we seem to have gone from repressed expressions of social complexity in the nineteenth century to a contemporary situation in which individuals and interest groups place overwhelming emphasis on their own self images as adequate response to reality. In both cases there has been a diminished expression of the public.

Recent participatory workshops where problems of urban design have been resolved show how several viewpoints can be reflected to give a more wholistic vision of reality. Parties can start together and evolve consensus and agreements about what should happen. Each may not get everything it wants but can realize why and how decisions were made. These procedures have shown people how to produce solutions that transcend obsessive self images.

For the creative architect, too, the image of one who indulges primarily in self expression will not be suitable for armatures. In *Artists and People,* a book applying to architects as well as artists, Su Braden tells about recent programs in Great Britain to make the arts more integral to society by having artists work in community contexts. Theory, she finds, is quickly re-

A segment of a large complex of student buildings for the medical faculty of the French-speaking University of Louvain, in Brussels. Reacting against institutional rigidities in the late sixties and against an architecture imposed by a single designer (symbolized by the building in the background of the left photograph), Lucien Kroll, architect, assisted student users through a complex process of programming, planning and construction, making possible a high degree of participation and self-help building. Kroll describes his role as organizer and leader: "I don't think the participants could have formed themselves into teams spontaneously and order the various retreats and the new attacks that were necessary. The animator is indispensible. My role in relation to those of the others was certainly not that of the traditional creator who makes all the decisions alone. It was that of an orchestrator and not a one-man band." The two photos (center and right) show students working out their version of a "flowing masonry buttress" whose size and location has been determined with the architect. The unexpected and "crude" form of the buttress jars our sensibilities while commenting on the administrative and economic difficulties of expressing poetic urges in orthodox architecture. The buttress creates an image of the building growing out of the earth and perhaps refers to a Jungian overlapping of foundations and cellars from previous buildings. (*Photo courtesy of Atelier Lucien Kroll, Architect, Bruxelles.*)

placed by actual experience; only through actively engaging with a community can artists acquire a perception of reality which matches that of ordinary people in local contexts. She points out that the structural base for artistic expression lies more accurately in the relationship between form and *context* than between form and content. Braden documents the problems artists with years of training and experience in gallery art and academia must face when working in any medium in a community.

By the often painful process of abandoning their self-absorbed involvement with the arts, artists come to understand that art in a community has to be *necessary action,* not merely an amenity brought in by outsiders. Even more importantly, the community, sometimes poor and with little or no connection to established arts, comes to recognize through working with artists that art and architecture can serve their needs as a free and democratic force. The new architect or artist may be likened to a producer. Success depends on finding new structures for designer-client relationships. To respond to citizens, architects will be willing to modify their aesthetic vocabulary and citizens in turn will gain confidence that the architect can serve their best interests by helping them find appropriate physical space for their involvement.

In our heterogeneous, mobile society with its many choices of technologies and materials, architects can render a profound service by find-

S. Giorgio Maggiore, Venice. Viewed from across the canal, the campanile and the continuation of the lower pediment through the façade, which were Scamozzi's contributions, do much to make the convincing and highly pictorial image. The campanile harmonizes with Palladio's dramatically tall classical columns, and the horizontal line of the pediment restates the long cornice line of the brick section of the church behind the façade. Palladio would probably have pulled out the four columns of the high pediment to create a three-dimensional portico, according to a revised plan he made in the mid-1570s. What was actually built by Scamozzi 35 years later, while in vigorous relief, nonetheless reads as a flat plane. The flat wall plane bounding a public space is an archetypal Italian urban form harmonizing with adjoining buildings. (*Photo by Phyllis Dearborn Massar.*)

ing degrees of order for extensive possibilities. In addition to the evolving role of producer, experience of trained professionals will be required to help determine where armatures are placed and how they fit into urban areas. Projections for future growth, engineering and management, the artistic and technical problems of assemblage, weathering and other aspects of building will also require professional skills. But the main point is that unlike heroic, virtuoso architects, the architect of an armature will be willing to see his or her form modified. He or she will realize that the nature of the armature is to change gradually while retaining enough of its distinguishing features so that its meaning and cultural associations assure continuity. If elements of the framework are particularly effective or loved they will be preserved for the same reasons society has kept other valued buildings. The architect for an armature will be an instinctive conservationist because the most important metaphor of the basic structure is one of continuity-in-time. To understand what our society has been, is, and what it might be, the architect will acquire knowledge of political and cultural history and how these have shaped architecture in the past. If a non-authoritarian architecture made up of a collage of citizens' works is intended, then commissions in which the design is set by an authoritarian decision-making process will be rejected. It is possible that in reaction to the predominant plainness of recent architecture, we may see a style of stuck-on additions and decorations from different periods that are in no way decided on nor contributed by users or citizen artists, nor held together by some unifying metaphor. By contrast, in an armature way of building, pastiche is to be avoided.

The designer of an armature will welcome the fact that future generations of designers will continue the work. In the past, when buildings were constructed to last over centuries and sometimes took decades to finish, it was inevitable that one architect would build sequentially on another's work. Some buildings done by famous architects have become what they are through the creativity of more than one architect. For example, S. Giorgio Maggiore in Venice is a church erected by Scamozzi in 1607–10 from Palladio's model of 1565.

Not only do architects contribute successfully to the work of earlier generations, but famous architects have often collaborated with a contemporary or responded to others' suggestions. Security Bank and Trust Co. at Owatonna, Minnesota, counted among the finest works of Louis Sullivan, was influenced by suggestions from his assistant, George Emslie.

The rise of private feelings as the ultimate denominator of creative experience has shaped architecture, especially in our own time when

Security Bank and Trust Co., Owatonna, Minnesota, Louis Sullivan, architect. The single arch on the street façade, which expresses the main banking room, seems an obvious and satisfying solution. Yet it was probably George Elmslie, Sullivan's assistant, who suggested that one large arch would be more appropriate than the three smaller ones in Sullivan's original design. This is not to say that Elmslie designed the building. The proportions, ornament, color and general handling all show evidence of Sullivan's originality. (*Photo by GEKS.*)

buildings are frequently identified by the name of the architect alone. However, the idea of artistic masterpieces having to be the creation of a single individual is a relatively late development in Western culture. It was the romantic tradition that fostered the notion of artists who overthrow the fetters of society and either by inspiration or patient labor produce great works, all-of-a-piece, owing little or nothing to circumstance beyond the control of the artist. This is a misleading interpretation. More than one architect, as well as chance and circumstance, are often instrumental in producing the assemblage of cues and contexts which we recognize as a great image.

To illustrate how imagination might be stimulated by the powerful work of another architect, I have made a sketch based on the ruin of Frank Lloyd Wright's Pauson House as the in-spiration for an armature large enough to form the nucleus for a small town. Wright's wall masses of concrete infilled with colorful stones picked from the Arizona desert echo the surrounding mountains, dramatically intersect the sky, and evoke memories of the communal pueblos of the Anasazi, ancient Indian inhabitants of the Southwest. It is an image that combines a variety of symbols, the synthesis of which is poetry.

The Pauson House is an example of the quality of suggestion and open-endedness offered by a ruin. The fact that the house is no longer a house, is no longer complete, inspires my imagination to fulfill the ruin's promise, to adapt it to my interpretation of a contemporary community. At the same time the image of the ruin is still there, not covered up, but remaining as a stable element within the overall de-

Ruins of the Pauson house, burned 1941, destroyed 1980. Paradise Valley, Arizona. Frank Lloyd Wright, architect. Wright created contrasting tensions in an architecture rooted to the earth and yet free of it. The humanly-scaled yet powerfully proportioned forms seem to grow from the desert like some natural outcrop, while the long horizontal terrace acts as a prow and makes a strong metaphor of a ship moving across the desert. (*Photo by Jeffrey Cook.*)

24

Drawing of armature based on the ruin of Frank Lloyd Wright's Pauson House. Branching out from the dark mass of the armature are sloping planes for solar collectors and greenhouses, alternating with terraces for dwellings of indeterminate design. The poetic intention, based on Wright's reference base of earth, ship, pueblo, is only the beginning of a scarcely imagined program for a site in the Southwestern United States. In the armature-ruin (shaded area) enclosed spaces are intended to house community functions while surfaces are gradually impressed with citizens' art (*Drawing by Herb Greene.*)

sign. Other designers might respond to the ruin in other ways and yet the basic image with its overlay of meanings would still remain.

I am asking that the architect give these same qualities to *new* structures which will bring forth a creative response in future designers and citizen artists. It is possible for a reference frame such as "ruin" to co-exist in a form that has a capacity for several other meanings. While it is important that the ruin reference not be so vague that interest is dissipated, still, if the reference is too blatant there is insufficient stimulus to the imagination. Many say we can't physically and should not ethically build instant ruins, but this is to misconstrue the intent. I'm saying we can reconstitute the image of ruin which suggests that there was once more to the structure and that there could be more than we now see. Architects from Alberti to Maybeck to SITE (Sculpture in the Environment) have utilized images of ruins which let us compare an imagined past with a corporeal present. Such a structure can be technically safe and visually stimulating with spaces provided for infilling. Painted surfaces, planted vines, (effective as sun shades), the sculptural form of the structure and the color and textures of back-up wall materials can sustain interest until more elaborate additions are realized.

In designing a long-lasting armature we can incorporate qualities often found in older buildings that give us a state of well-being. These are defined by Patrick Horsbrugh, by the term "energesis." Tactile comfort, the sense of security, stimulation of the imagination, preferred scale and color ambience are among the difficult-to-measure factors. As we began to find new uses for older buildings in the 1970s, many pre-Modern mills, warehouses, schools and other structures built of stone, masonry and heavy timber were found to possess energesic values to a higher degree than is usually found in later buildings. The scale and texture of stones, the rhythm and detail of windows, the sound, smell and resilience of heavy timber floors, combine to make space inside, not the abstract space of the International Modern style, but a tangible, palpable space. The goal of the architect for an armature is to find new poetic images that, like Wright's Pauson House ruin, draw us to the building over the centuries and which incorporate energesic qualities in their new spaces and forms.

Faneuil Hall Marketplace, Boston, Massachusetts. Historic stone warehouses act as a basic framework to which later, lighter buildings have been added. Much contemporary architecture, with its bar joists, dropped ceilings, impoverished textures and oversimplified forms would not be worth recycling for such a use. For the future, why not build basic armatures that incorporate both the strength of image and the loose fit suggested by these warehouse buildings? (*Photos by Nanine Hilliard Greene.*)

The Architect for a Background Architecture

The term "background architecture" is usually taken to mean a vernacular of modest character that acts as a backdrop to life or to selected pieces of dramatic architecture. What I am describing for armatures is more analogous to paintings of the Western world in which backgrounds are enlivened to suggest what Alfred North Whitehead calls a sense of imminence, that-which-is-about-to-be, as if the figures in the foreground are linked to their setting in time and space, giving the whole a connection to past, present and future, a kind of causality. The deep space of Rembrandt's paintings, charged with warmth and incident, is possibly the most potent example.

An armature, acting as a background architecture, will have to support bursts of vividly detailed expressions from participating artists and citizen-craftspersons. I do not mean unassuming physical support but a structure itself as full of positive interest as Gaudi's undulating bench in the Parc Guëll. Small in size though this example may be, it is a powerfully expressive image of the biological energy which the philosopher Henri Bergson, Gaudi's contemporary, characterized as *élan vital*.

The designer of the armature frame will seek backgrounds of energetic quality that have the capability of holding and directing attention without being too specific. These backgrounds will be capable of many interpretations by a heterogeneous society possessing an increasing ability for reading expressive form. They will accommodate timely intrusions and comment and simultaneously accept timeless works of art. By their formal organization, armatures-as-backgrounds become symbols of interconnection and are therefore unifying contexts for highly indeterminate additions. Just as the expression of deep space evolved in the Baroque period and has continued to the present, I foresee the evolution of symbolic conventions expressing the continuum of time and space as well as the perceptual processes which make us aware of the continuum's existence.

I am saying we can have a field which can be a wall, paving, background or form of any kind, that gives cues of connectivity. Far more than a neutral backdrop, I am speaking of a continuum that contains and pulls together anything citizen artists may think of so that what seems diverse is actually a part of the physical continuum of matter appearing and reappearing in

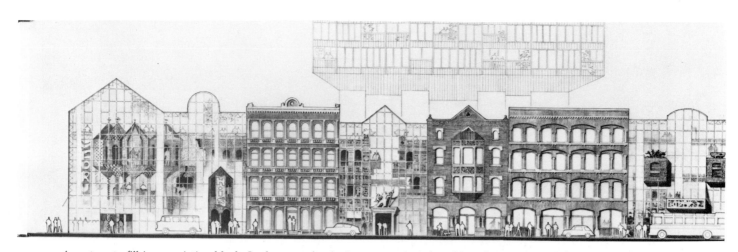

Armature to fill in an existing block. In the core of today's cities we often find usable old buildings standing between vacant lots where derelict or unprofitable structures have been torn down—often for more profitable parking lots. To reconstitute a block, this armature combines preservation of historic structures with a ghost image of lost buildings made by the profile of a glassed galleria that permits the development of fanciful structures inside without the constraint of making them waterproof. Interior framework can respond to the materials, openings, colors, proportions and other design characteristics of the adjacent existing buildings. Incorporated within an image of their former block, older buildings give strength to an accessible symbol of nostalgia while leaving users space for additions in an unknown future. (*Drawing by Herb Greene.*)

Detail of armature to fill in an existing block. Craftsmen working on the interior of the armature and people shopping at the market inside or attending other functions can be seen by passersby, adding to the life of the street. The transparent gallery, not necessarily air conditioned, can be ventilated by large sliding doors at street level and windows at key positions to provide natural circulation of air. Exhaust fans augment breeze, and canvas shades provide decorative sun control. In winter, space heaters in key positions and passive solar heating can make the galleria comfortable much of the day. (*Drawing by Herb Greene.*)

27

different forms as science has revealed. The collage form of armatures can express this cosmology: the organic philosophy that nothing is lost, that everything is utilized and that each incident can find its place. If this expression in an armature is powerful enough, then even the kitsch and trivial will be encompassed. Suspended and coordinated against this symbolic background, these details can vivify by contrast and become poignant and affecting. When really outstanding folk art comes along it deserves to be seen in the public realm. In fact there are few works of art that can't be set off more effectively by an appropriate background. The reigning perception is that a work of art should tell us nothing but about itself. But I believe a piece of art is extensive: an architectural background, with the right cues, can bring enhanced meanings to the work and in turn receive meaning.

An armature comes to full fruition as encrustations of the many are added to strongly metaphoric images initiated by the architect. No longer will the architect say through his or her work, "This building is a summary of myself," but rather, "I become myself as you make *your* contribution."

We have yet to experience first rank architects designing strong images that invite an ongoing democratic process of citizen additions. But if an armature of both dense images and of collage is our intention, the architect will of necessity become more poet than business person, more service- than ego-oriented. To create the open-ended form in a spirit of cooperation that is intrinsic to the concept, architects will need to evolve into background generalists in a profound, not falsely modest, sense and will appreciate that the mature expression of one's own design is its ability to attract and support creative contributions from others over generations and centuries.

Antonio Gaudi's bench in the Parc Güell, Barcelona. Even without its marvelous mosaic surface, this bench would be a strong image. In this metaphor of pulsing life, we see images of waves, of curves that remind us of life and organisms. Gaudi was not only able to project a sense of organism in images of universal significance, he was able to leave the surface open-ended to the particular, to patterns of broken tile (the local "waste material") that reflects in its white color field and its blues and greens the Mediterranean sand, sky and sea and in its vivid reds and oranges the flowers of Catalonian street vendors. We know that many of these brilliant mosaic designs were created by Gaudi's assistants. The unique contribution of a designer to an armature is the creation of this degree of power in a background architecture that is still open to the work of others. (*Drawing by Herb Greene.*)

3 Toward Symbolic Roots

As I walk through the main square of the armature there is power in the mass and sense of envelopment—not the power of an authority or an elite but an aesthetic power made by richness and strength of material, by the accumulation of people's craftwork and by a resemblance to natural form. Centuries of architectural geology and human history have come together to give solemnity to this place. Yet the solemnity dissolves into bursts of color and action. I can see people at work on fanciful reliefs. A market with banners, painted stalls and translucent roofs makes a kaleidoscope. Street players perform on a stage integral with the armature building. On the square is a castle made of paper flowers, a float left over from yesterday's parade. The square is a spatial theater full of disparate events. Its signs of continuity suggest that all the people and props within it are accepted in an enfolding whole.

SOME claim that the new perception of environment as a changing flow of information transmitted by electronic media has removed the need for symbolic buildings as we have known them in the past. Futurists present us with images of mass populations living in nomadic environments made up of demountable capsules and pods connected by television.

Disregarding practical problems, this prospect would seem to diminish our contact with the natural and the historic world and tie us irrevocably to the questionable instrument of smoothly functioning hardware. I'm not suggesting that outdoor films, light-and-sound shows, teletype and television receivers might not be built into public armatures, but rather that there are values to long-lasting traditionally symbolic architecture that can never be substituted for by the transfer of image or idea by electronic means alone. As Ruskin affirmed, architecture has lasting, expressive powers and symbolic value; architecture can connect forgotten and following ages with each other. I believe such an architecture is reliable and accessible. Unlike mechanical equipment which may fail, it is visible to individuals at any time, day or night, in all kinds of weather and through the various perspectives of each individual soul.

My own belief is that we cannot do without fixed symbols analogous to important buildings, from Luxor to Ronchamp. These landmarks provide the detached, dispassionate object, free from the contingencies of motion, vacillating tastes, and the attitudes of broadcasters. Allowing for differences in interpretation, buildings in their symbolic role give us access to our natural retrieval system—the mind. Through the selective reconstitution of historical types, integrated with successful expressions of fresh ideals, images in buildings encompass meanings far beyond the capabilities of automated storage systems. Our imagination extends its vision by seeing one thing in terms of another, by making unlikely connections. It is the nature of the mind rather than computers to see metaphors in architectural forms. Therefore, a long-lasting armature becomes an icon to which to attach uncoerced symbolic meanings. I use the word icon purposefully with all its connotations of idol and fixity. It is this fixed and stable quality intrinsic to architecture that I believe cannot be substituted for. Hopefully the symbolic content of an armature would reveal to a community some eternal value in the passage of daily lives.

I believe that there are roots, common to all humanity, from which positive symbols may be created. The architect's obligation is to sense these origins and to give them form. Three that I would like to discuss as basic themes for armatures are root images of historic continuity; images of public participation; and images of an ecological relationship between humankind and nature.

"For, indeed, the greatest glory of a building is not in its stones, nor in its gold. Its glory is in its Age, and in that deep sense of voicefulness, of stern watching, of mysterious sympathy, nay, even of approval or condemnation, which we feel in walls that have long been washed by the passing waves of humanity. It is in their lasting witness against men, in their quiet contrast with the transitional character of all things, in the strength which, through the lapse of seasons and times, and the decline and birth of dynasties, and the changing of the face of the earth, and of the limits of the sea, maintains its sculptured shapeliness for a time insuperable, connects forgotten and following ages with each other, and half constitutes the identity, as it concentrates the sympathy, of nations: it is in that golden stain of time, that we are to look for the real light, and colour, and preciousness of architecture; and it is not until a building has assumed this character, till it has been entrusted with the fame, and hallowed by the deeds of men, till its walls have been witnesses of suffering, and its pillars rise out of the shadows of death, that its existence, more lasting as it is than that of the natural objects of the world around it, can be gifted with even so much as these possess, of language and of life."

John Ruskin

In many frontier towns, buildings were insubstantial and hastily built. The opening of the frontier, the founding of small scale communities where the individual counted, and the romance of distant horizons let us ascribe poetic values to these villages. The urban form of many downtowns evolved from beginnings like Main Street, Wasco, Oregon, about 1890. (*Photo by W. A. Raymond. Courtesy The Bettman Archive, Inc.*)

A century later we have returned to insubstantial buildings more interesting as cardboard models presented by architects to corporation boards than as built pieces of urban fabric. A convention center, hotel and office tower, Lexington, Kentucky, located a block away from Main Street, illustrate how the original urban form has been lost, eaten away by parking lots, without establishing new form. (*Photo by Nanine Hilliard Greene.*)

The solidarity and detail of vintage architecture is giving way to the thin, flat, curtain wall economics of the present. In an armature program old buildings that have to be torn down because of structural inadequacy or obsolete program might retain a semblance of an aesthetic "ruin" by selective protection of key features, corners and details. (*Photo by Nanine Hilliard Greene.*)

Le Corbusier's Notre Dame du Haut, Ronchamp, France. The roof, great in size and aspiring in contour, is redolent with associations of European thatch roofs and with other objects that refer to peasants and religious articles, such as arks and nun's hats. This non-Euclidean roof shape, a form connoting relativity and the synthesis of space-time, would seem to belie reference to familiar objects, yet the very freedom of this shape from particular instance helps suspend us in that most vital realm of artistic accomplishment—dialogue between the particular and the universal. We are able to move from "peasant roof" to aspiring symbol.

The walls, here incorporating a mass of on-site rubble from an earlier church destroyed by the Nazis, recall other walls rich in history as defense against invasion and a harsh climate. (*Photo courtesy Hunter Adams Architecture Library, University of Kentucky.*)

Reincarnating the Past: Images of Historic Continuity

Before and since the arrival of Europeans, North America has produced very few long-lasting buildings. Constant rapid growth of our towns and cities has encouraged expedient, cheap, light-weight architecture easily torn down and replaced with something different as new needs have arisen. So lavish have we been with our resources that even well-built, handsome and serviceable structures have gone down in the name of "modernization." Six or seven buildings have stood on the same site in many of our city centers in less than two hundred years. Because of rising costs new buildings have an aura of impermanence, reinforced by the likelihood that owners will raze them as soon as it becomes profitable. In designated historic districts, this is now more difficult and no longer as economically profitable, but the trend continues in the center city and in new suburbs. It may be difficult for Europeans with their long centuries of sturdy buildings still standing to understand how widespread is the transience and instability of the architecture of many new world towns. However, even in Europe, new towns, redeveloped housing, and the new suburbs of old cities frequently have the same atmosphere as American towns: an absence of historic architecture to which emotional attachments can be made. Many towns in developing countries suffer, too, from this same sense of rootlessness.

To counteract this rootlessness in an armature framework, I propose that valued historic forms be reconstituted. As an illustration of poetic reconstitution Le Corbusier, in the chapel of Notre Dame du Haut at Ronchamp, has reconstituted familiar historic features of tower, wall and roof with such perceptual clarity, force and richness of expressive cues that they appear to us as archetypes. And, as corresponding emotions are experienced, the viewer feels a sudden sense of recognition. Rather than a work of hermetic indulgence, Ronchamp warrants our careful attention as we see historic references that were inadmissible by the International Style of the 1920's, and that were forgotten during the proliferation of much memoryless modern construction. With the destruction of so much of the older architectural fabric in American cities, we now feel an ever increasing need for this continuity with history.

Some of my richest experiences of architecture have been initiated by complex and highly developed buildings that carry visible traces of a remote and imagined past. In the Mayan City of Uxmal, for example, the form of many of the temples is visibly derived from the form of the earliest house. Sculptural details on the façades sometimes actually imitate the image of the little house. Similarly the aedicula, a little shrine, a sort of architectural canopy or rudimentary temple complete with pediment that can be traced to Hellenistic and Roman times, is a recurring theme in Gothic, Renaissance and Modern architecture. The repetition of the miniature building suggests a psychological need for intimacy and ceremony. I would also guess that the recurrent image of the little house in examples of world architecture is more than an atrophied symbol. It is a necessary device to bring the present in contact with the past, to recall childhood experiences and to give evidence of earlier generations to which people need to be linked in order to develop the sense of belonging to a stream of life with origins in a remote time often imagined as idyllic. The sign of idyllic or settled past seems to create hope and conviction that there will be a meaningful future. This enduring motive for expressing the past in connection with the present seems necessary for civilization. Provision for this sort of empathy, undervalued and nearly eliminated by most Modern architecture, I am treating as a primary determinant of form.

In criticizing the Modern or International, I realize that the core of many cities is comprised of new buildings in this style. While I have never embraced Modern because of its lack of regional response and other ideological inadequacies, I believe its failures are more a consequence of the way architects have used it than because of the style itself. I believe we can integrate armatures into settings with the Modern in a way that will return permanence and a sense of history to cities. And in reverse, we can establish long-lasting armatures so that the Modern, which is likely to be continued as a style but which often tends to be neutral or a-historical, can be seen in contrast to the armature and by association be anchored in time and place.

Other conditions that maintain contact with valued origins are pointed out by René Dubos, the eminent microbiologist, who believes that human life is conditioned by a biological as well as cultural past. He connects this past to the persistence of regionalism. Speaking about the sense of place he says, "Regionalism has an enduring justification in the cosmic, terrestrial and historic characteristics of each particular place. Because it is rooted in both human and physical nature, environmental diversity will persist within the political ecumenism of One World. Natural and cultural forces will overcome technological and political imperatives and continue to nurture the genius loci which accounts for the persistence of place." Dubos is saying that place has a physical and chemical foundation. As soils and vegetation can express place so can architecture and observing indigenous architecture can disclose important links to place. A biological and cultural basis of regional color differences offers a model for armatures to strengthen ties to place through the reconstitution of color cues. Color in architecture, restricted by the Reformation, undermined by neoclassic taste and Cartesian attitudes and overwhelmed by industrialism in the eighteenth and nineteenth centuries, is among the most important qualities of architecture.

Tobacco barn, Fayette County, Kentucky. Barns painted black to absorb heat for drying tobacco, and ventilators painted white, have become regional landmarks in the Bluegrass area. (*Photo by Nanine Hilliard Greene.*)

The Unitarian Church of Lexington, Lexington, KY. Herb Greene, architect, 1965. Black stain on a mass of cedar siding and white painted steel trusses give this suburban church a degree of regional identity. (*Photo by Bill Strode.*)

Color not only influences our well-being directly through sensation but by linking a matrix of cultural and physical factors establishes ties to a local region. Buildings that incorporate images or evoke memories of an area's biological and cultural past will thus be unique and diverse and will be in tune with the organic particularities of human and physical nature.

Recycling and rehabilitating old buildings points to another example of protecting origins (although the spiraling costs of new construction have provoked much of this interest). Unfortunately, a great deal of useable building stock was unnecessarily demolished during the era of cheap energy and expedient economic expansion. However, the proliferation of preservation societies and the funding of preservation projects with government and private monies indicates that reasons for preservation go beyond economic gain. American urban renewal has been destructive of the fabric of the city and has wiped out the social and psychological values of place, time, ancestral ties and character, qualities difficult to incorporate in most new construction.

We are now discovering that many buildings built before the reductionist standards of 1945–1965 have features that make them satisfying to recycle. I refer to their scale, rhythm, materials, details and other characteristics. When we become aware of these we can feel what it meant to be alive in the time contemporary to the form. In the Georgian style, for instance, the rhythmic use of columns, windows and dormers is comparable to the rhythmic symmetries of eighteenth century European music and gives us important information about attitudes and feelings of those who produced the work, and provides a dialectic to our own feelings and attitudes. As we walk in older buildings, it is not only the built shapes that link us with the past but the immediate sense of the presence of people long gone, of mythical beings, of events recalled.

Most scientific and materialist doctrine assumes that people no longer need to think or feel this way. Some might say that the thousands who saw the television production, *Roots,* simply set off afterwards to trace their earliest known ancestors to count and name them with detached objectivity. Ernst Cassirer, the noted philosopher, would have said they were seeking better knowledge of themselves and of the present in the "mythical past." Old usages, institutions, interests and individual acts embodied and symbolized by the composition of artifacts and armature are hallowed by their integration with a mythical past. The armature focuses our interest in the artifacts' existence and encourages our understanding of their teleology.

I believe architecture is ripe for an imaginative reconstitution of historical forms. I do not mean the use of "colonial" pediments and mansard roofs on Ramada Inns and endless apartments. Nor do I mean the archaeological reconstruction of Williamsburg windows, dormers, brickwork, etc. They are not metaphorical nor reconstituted in forms that are themselves a fresh expression of a modern program. They almost invariably produce kitsch or at best a museum atmosphere as in Williamsburg. Rather, the aim is to provide regional resources and selections from the collective memory to weave our work into a richer texture of time frames. The ideals of Modern architecture stressed an abstract, formal unity integrated with machine production. The inclusion of period furniture or fragments of historic architecture was an anathema to many advocates of pure Modern who in reaction to an eclectic approach to history insisted that both buildings and furnishings should reflect only the new machine age time. The whole range of scholarly and sensual combinations between machine and craft technologies and old and new forms was usually overlooked. I see the acceptance of a clash between time frames in an image as an exciting aesthetic possibility.

"Corridart," a street exhibition and art fair—Montreal, 1976. Melvin Charney, artist-architect. A plywood mockup of former buildings lost to a parking lot indicates the kind of research that could be pertinent in finding local origins for the forms and materials of armatures. As a study in archeology, the displays along this Montreal street included photo-murals of significant buildings and pageants, and of people who had formed the neighborhood. (*Photo courtesy of Melvin Charney.*)

A mural of the Davis, California, Landmark Arch, 1916–1922. Bicentennial project 1976 by T. E. Buckendorf (Copyright 1976). An illusion in an unexpected place, this 1920s arch, incarnating a lost landmark, lifts a parking lot into an aesthetic overlap of time. Painted on the end wall of a downtown building, the arch is a gateway to the past that opens horizons which suggest a stream of space and time, in front as well as behind us. (*Photo by Nanine Hilliard Greene.*)

Currently we are getting more examples of deliberate mismatches in time frames as vintage buildings are being rehabilitated for new uses. The challenge to architects is to develop appropriate contrasts to the old building that they are recycling. Most contemporary examples settle for keeping features of the old while treating their additions as neutral or as expressions of the current exposed duct, hard edge geometry and flat color style. Imagination and sensitivity will be needed to transcend style and produce a correspondence of feeling between past and present. The razing of many urban structures has left exposed masonry walls with ghosts of bricked-in windows, stairs, partitions and other traces of use and habitation. Some of the unplanned leftovers of urban demolition are visually more interesting than much new construction. It would seem possible to integrate the best of these palimpsests into new architecture even at some inconvenience to a program. Saving remnant walls can sometimes cut costs and add character.

Many architects prefer references to machines in their buildings. They see a building as another machine like a ship or plane or typewriter whose parts move and which is movable in space. Unlike a plane or ship, architecture which remains tied to a particular place, can reveal the acts of preceding generations who have created it. Old architectural forms can even have a positive influence in shaping new institutions, as, for example, the Benedictine order which originally settled in the courtyards of rural villas and responded by adapting these to become cloisters. Sherban Cantacuzino suggests that monastic planning might have taken a different course if villas had not been available. Functions change and projections often overlook some aspect of the problem that intrudes after the architecture has been solidified in concrete. Perhaps the most important generic architectural type for the future will be the building that can be changed and added to and yet provides a vital reference base in both historical and existential values so that its reuse becomes a heartfelt need.

"Stairways," the Junior League Building, Louisville, Kentucky. This three-story brick-walled gallery is sandwiched between two of a series of nineteenth century mercantile buildings with exceptionally fine cast iron façades. Several years ago a fire gutted the floors of the original building, now remodeled for use as display, meeting and office space. The textural quality of the old brick wall, the abstract patterns made by corbelling used to support wooden beams, and the rhythms of the voids once enclosed by the wooden floors are fascinating. The depth of interest stems not from abstract pattern alone but from the sense of use by people of a previous time. An architect coordinating an armature workshop program could lead citizen artists in designing and building lighting, seating and paving that might be specifically sensitive to the space, materials and historic associations of the building. Ubiquitous catalog furniture and light fixtures, necessitated by economics, are a harsh choice in many design situations. (*Shulhafer/Wright, architects. Larry E. Wright, Project Architect. Photo by Steve Barry.*)

To illustrate how I have attempted to reconstitute historic forms into a contemporary building, I include here a farm house in Kentucky that reveals many references to a nearby Shaker Village.

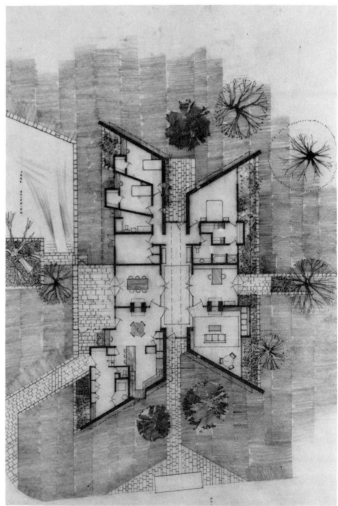

The French residence. Herb Greene, architect. In 1966 I designed a farm residence for admirers of Shaker architecture and furniture, whose property is not far from the restored Shaker Village at Pleasant Hill, Kentucky. The design reconstitutes a traditional high ceilinged central hall, with doors at both ends for cross ventilation during the hot Kentucky summers. Thick walls, small rooms and the generally symmetrical plan recapture the feeling of the solid buildings at Pleasant Hill. Dark stained, built-in cabinets; deep blue-green trim; and off-white plaster walls reflect the orderly, restrained Shaker influence. These details are combined with a spatial openness and sensitivity with light and scale that derives from the houses of Frank Lloyd Wright. As one walks through the rooms the mind picks up cues that evoke the lives of the Shakers, and simultaneously notices the twentieth century feel for continuous space that opens out into the green countryside. (*Photo by Bill Strode, drawing by Herb Greene.*)

Another example of historical form reconstituted into a contemporary building to strengthen a sense of place is a hypothetical public health center and bath designed as an armature next to a recently completed civic center in downtown Lexington, Kentucky.

In designing a "Roman Bath" in Lexington, I emphasize that this is not a case of replicating an entire historic building such as the Baths of Caracalla in miniature. I intend to express a contemporary program, keep the use of structure and materials reasonably honest, relate the building to the site and allow indeterminacy in the execution of surfaces and, to some degree, of the buildings' spaces as well. In and around Lexington many of the more notable buildings are ante-bellum mansions and townhouses. Frequently appearing are beaux arts versions of neo-Greek and Roman churches, banks, colleges and hospitals. Compared with Phoenix,

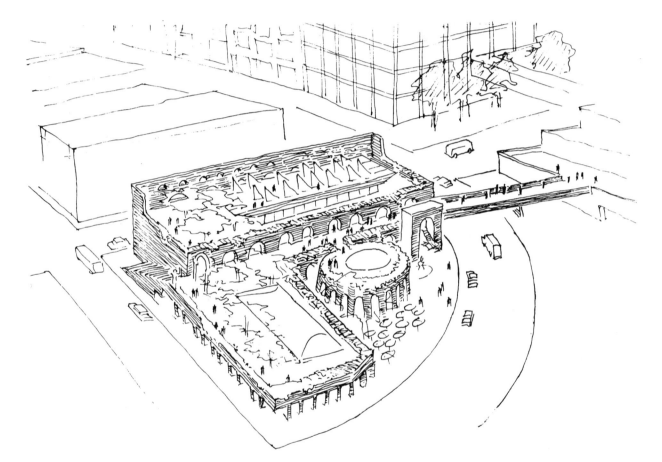

Armature for Health Center reconstituting Roman form in Lexington, Kentucky. The height and width of the building is a reflection of three-story buildings nearby. Behind the "Roman wall" will be seen a series of gardened terraces descending to the curved street facing the Civic Center (right). The higher part of the building can be used for saunas, exercise, dance, gymnastics, shops for exercise equipment and other health related functions. The circular building with columns, each different and of changing diameters, done by individual craftsmen, houses a health food and juice bar with sidewalk tables at street level and a roof garden above. The framework controls its general diameter and shape, moving from an approximation of a classical order to sloped piers influenced by Gaudi's famous columns in the Parc Güell. This transition from one column to another reinforces the image of continuum. The pseudo triumphal arch, broken away from the other structures so its partially exposed frame becomes a scaffolding for people's art, marks a stairway and houses a lift to the bridge, which is shown here in rudimentary form intended to invite redesign by others. On the second level, extending from the bridge, is a row of artists' studios and workshops, with rents subsidized by an agency of the public realm, as is done in Toronto's Eaton Place by the Art Commission of Canada. This second level is identifiable as a pedestrian street through the entire site and can become part of a new network of pedestrian spaces that will help recover the city from the automobile. Above the artist studios is a third level open rooftop with sunbathers sheltered from the wind by canvas "sails." (*Drawing by Herb Greene.*)

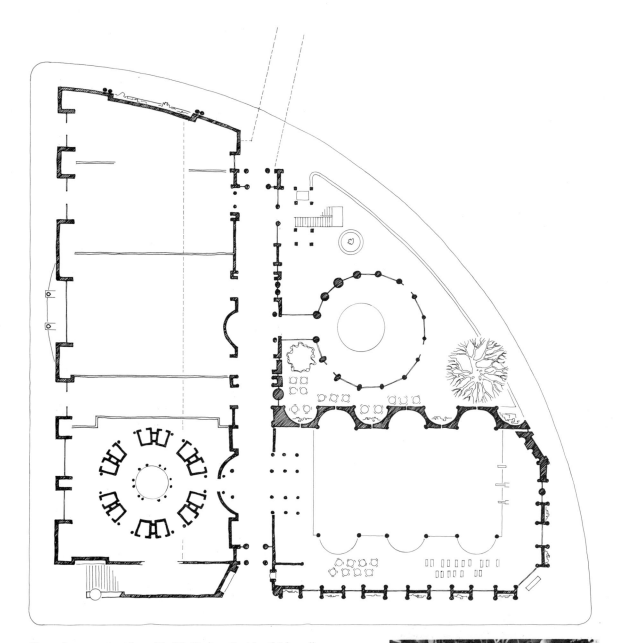

Plan of an armature for a Health Center. Inside, thick walls with circular niches, transcribed from the bath of Diocletian, surround the pool. Symmetrical colonnades at the entrance, the shape of the sauna baths and other details, give bathers a sense of the actual proportions, arrangements and phenomenal qualities of parts of a Roman bath. The saunas might be finished in redwood and mosaic tile, but they would closely follow the cross section profiles of Roman piers. The intention is not to build scale models of Roman fragments but to synthesize the sensual and intellectual aspects of the historical form with a contemporary program, keeping up a commentary for our enjoyment. (*Drawing by Herb Greene.*)

(*Right*) Madonna of the Bath. Peewee Valley, Kentucky. The cast iron bathtub with its arch-like curve, painted blue inside, becomes a niche for a mass-produced Madonna. Feelings evoked by this particular juxtaposition span seriousness, sentimentality and humor. This assemblage could be integrated in a continuum of reliefs in the public bath, together with other unexpected elements of kitsch, wit, scholarship and art. (*Photo by Nanine Hilliard Greene.*)

Arizona, for example, Lexington is dominated by English colonial buildings with a liberal sprinkling of Victorian, many of them "Italianized" with arched openings. Furthermore, when Kentucky was settled in the late 1700s, it was a territorial edge to the new Republic, and many of its mementos date from a neoclassic period when cultivated people idealized things Roman. Thomas Jefferson wrote a poem about the Maison Carré, a Roman temple in Nice. Houdon sculpted George Washington as a Roman Senator. At the time of the Civil War, Cassius was the name of one of Kentucky's most legendary abolitionists and a century later Cassius was the name of the state's famous prizefighter, Mohammed Ali. So there is a basis for Roman references because, mixed with ever-increasing shopping centers and other modern

Armature for a Health Center with Roman references. Elevation. The wall is actually a hollow sculptural form eight feet thick that allows options in construction and use. Formed to gain a sense of historical Roman mass, it creates a space within itself, as well as making alcoves and providing functional openings for pipes and structural supports. (*Drawing by Herb Greene.*)

Detail of an armature for a Health Center. A series of two-story arches was selected to allow for higher interior spaces. The proportions of the arch to the height of the building refers to the ponderous, stolid and often inert proportions of historic Roman architecture. Irregular spacing of the arches reflects the need for varying widths in the program, and a conscious manipulation to gain asymmetry. (The first study had tall, three story single arches with too much flavor of beaúx arts Roman.) For privacy, the arches can be closed in with translucent glass. The smaller, arched openings near the top are fairly obvious references to an aqueduct. Large arches indicate that the wall is a space-enclosing structure, with Roman antecedents juxtaposed with the reading of an aqueduct. References begin to include the importance of water for the bath, the legendary engineering skill of the Romans and the sheer bulk of an aqueduct with its near indestructibility, a source of wonder to the western world. (*Drawing by Herb Greene.*)

Left: Arch of Constantine, Rome, A.D. 12. (*Photo, College of Architecture Archives, University of Kentucky.*) *Center:* A Roman arch entrance gate to a 1907 residential court. The proportions may be weak but the stone is real and the arch has a presence. (*Photo by Nanine Hilliard Greene.*) *Right:* Plywood Roman. Thin sheets and thinner historicism are used to "classicize" a 1970s builder's apartment. (*Photo by Nanine Hilliard Greene.*)

buildings, people still see various offshoots of Rome in their daily lives. Of course one might insist on a thoroughly archaeological approach and trace the Roman architectural forms back, in our Lexington baths, to the Greeks but Rome was famous for the institution of the bath. Although associated with debauchery and lassitude that supposedly contributed to the downfall of the empire, the baths were also known for their libraries and therapeutic aids. Because they provide a treasury of associations derived from tales of Caesar, Gibbon and Hollywood, they make an intriguing, historic sounding board. Along with aqueducts and colosseums, Roman baths are among the architectural images most deeply embedded in American memories of ancient history.

It is my feeling that the Roman reference should be accessible to a broad spectrum of people. This does not mean acceptance of the kitsch images that decorate a developer's hotel such as Caesar's Palace in Las Vegas, but that people who are not architects and scholars are privy to recognizable signs included in the primary impact of the building. The current recovery of history attempted by some leading post-Modern architects often reverts to a specialist's set of references. For instance, these references are often derived from the vocabulary of flat planes and ship railings of Modern architecture in the 1920's and from fragments of a classical architecture appreciated by architects, critics and patrons themselves, more as signs of an intellectual elitism than as touchstones for the popular imagination and for regional sensitivity. It is possible to provide an architectural framework that includes references with both popular and scholarly meanings.

Brick is the predominant material in the facing of the armature baths. This is not the long thin structural brick of Roman buildings but a veneer made up of shades of the red brick which predominate in Kentucky and are used to transfer regional colors and scale to the new structure. Brick is also chosen as workable for a citizen's craft program in which a variety of colors and patterns would be employed by artisans expressing various degrees of individuality. The mosaics and textures would be the outgrowth of individual expression within a framework of designated color harmonies and surface forms. The surfaces of many modern buildings lose their gloss soon after completion. The mottled brick work on the Health Center is intended to age. Stains and color changes will not destroy its surface but will help establish the valued reference frame of age and act as a counterpoint to later additions which may employ stainless materials and synthetic finishes that resist weathering. Stimulated by the reconstitution of historic forms, it is intended for people to make unpredictable metaphoric connections not determined by the architect. History, I believe, is one of our most fertile sources for the generation of powerful images. It is the opportunity of the architect to understand which historic roots can be used in the armature frame that will deeply touch a community.

Without emotional attachment, citizens cannot be expected to cherish their built environment nor creatively contribute to it.

Images of "The Public"

As people work together and see the results of their work, I foresee an armature becoming the symbol of the public place to meet. The buildings, streets, markets, residential cul-de-sacs and walkways in, around and connected to an urban armature will be rich in places for face-to-face encounters. The city is our primary instrument of human communication. Multifarious and subtle human transactions do not lend themselves to TV images and notation that are as satisfying as direct encounters. One of the powerful meanings of an armature at the core of a city will be a new image and definition of "public." Through armatures I am trying to find a way to make a basic framework, particularly for public buildings, so that their stability invites the small scale. Together the stable and the improvised become the image of a society that can agree to certain important symbols and yet remain open to individual expression which may or may not support these meanings.

As an image of the gathered-together public, the architectural and ornamental diversity within an armature framework should parallel and accept the presence of differences, or mismatches, among things, individuals and groups within the body politic of a democracy. While an armature is intended as a practical building in which heterogeneous people will work and socialize, it may find its most profound use as a symbolic object for dispelling our usually unfounded sense of being threatened by what is different in things and in other human beings. One of our learned or perhaps inherited characteristics is the ability to recognize quickly a feature in our surroundings that does not fit with the background we have organized in our minds. On an armature, collage and surrealistic ornament derived from unexpected combinations of people's art, seen against a stable background, can provide us with real, visible surprises on which to exercise our talent for spotting the unexpected and on which to focus our sense of being threatened by what or who is different. If our fears can be defused in cathartic feelings that place the "dangerous" in context, then surprising conjunctions can be recognized as non-threatening. Perhaps one of the reasons why so-called rational architecture elicits so little affection and allegiance from most people is that its lack of surprises prevents us from exercising this innate alarm system. And, too, since each human personality in its layers below surface contains mismatches, our ultimate ennui toward so much current architecture modeled on the machine may stem from resistance to its message that it is so unlike ourselves. Quite opposite from limiting ourselves to increasing uniformity in architecture and in ways of living, an armature philosophy of building is intended to widen our recognition and tolerance of the unusual, the variegated, the indeterminate among people as well as things, and give these visible symbolic form.

I am suggesting it is the responsibility of the architect and the community in a pluralist society to seek out and build into public buildings these *intentionally positive* symbols of diversity and complexity. We can no longer afford to build public buildings whose images are contradictory to the professed ideals of our society, whether the messages they convey are unintentional, or even whether they are an accurate reflection of our imperfect state of affairs. We now see the authoritarianism in new cities such as Brasilia or in the echelon of recent state office buildings at Albany, New York, which were supposedly designed to symbolize the "progressive" but whose hi-tech, slick forms, monumentality and regimented rhythms legitimize the power of official élites and at the same time point to the vulnerability of non-élites. We can't afford to repeat architectural symbols of oppression and distrust since these act as unconscious beacons toward an authoritarian future. We need city halls and urban-county buildings with more complex images whose messages impart the sharing of power, the efficacy of the individual, and the accessibility of government combined with civic dignity and historic continuity. It is possible for an appropriate art image to include references to earlier types of architecture presently seen as negative, such as the fortress connotation of Boston's city hall, for example, but to be rele-

City Hall, Boston, Massachusetts. The image seems too coercive and unwelcoming for a building which should express government as servant of the people. An articulated, heavy and formidable structure, influenced by Le Corbusier's "fortress image" in the monastery of LaTourette, it is placed in a vast plaza nearly devoid of shelter except for a subway entrance. (So uniform is the expanse of brick paving that a barely visible pattern done by one non-conforming brick-layer was given an award as creative brickwork!) Even the trees in a small sitting area to one side and the intentionally free access to the building are not enough to dispel images of an unprotected citizenry facing a bastion that speaks of centralized, authoritarian power rather than of participation by citizens. (*Photo by Nanine Hilliard Greene.*)

vant to our times these cues need to be dissolved and overlaid by a more positive image of democratic government and individual decision making. Humanely-scaled amenities such as sitting places, shade, shelter and comfortable access can go a long way toward illustrating how a building and the institution inside are intended to relate to the citizenry.

Any place where people come to meet, whether a small neighborhood building or a block in the center of a city can become a symbol of community. An armature alive with the crafts and activity of the local men, women and children becomes a symbol of participation. A mosaic of citizens' work on a long-lived armature is a statement in itself that people are willing to work together and that they believe in the future enough to leave something for others to enjoy. The chance to contribute to something more permanent than ourselves gives each of us a touch of immortality, not through the egocentric pyramid of a Pharaoh but through a building symbolic of each individual's participation in the common stream of human life.

Through an armature we may see ourselves as part of a larger whole, of a group that together expresses a social entity whether a small neighborhood, a big city or, even more poignantly, our connection to all of humanity. Perhaps the image of a perfectly democratic state can be accomplished only by the accumulation of individual decisions and their small scale consequences. Yet, I believe the individual and the public whole, which encompasses our collective images, inextricably reinforce each other and have to be acknowledged in our buildings.

I see public armatures as inclusive rather than exclusive images. Working for specialized clients, we architects often become exclusive, having to limit our imaginations and cut ourselves off from the variety implied by "public," in order to satisfy a narrowly specific client—an insurance company, a denominational church or an exclusive resort. Even city halls and other buildings that belong to all of us have been given the guise of the bureaucracies inside them: we tend to think of "public" and "government" as synonymous. I see armatures sym-

43

An armature with related buildings that together scale down the architecture of a large city/county complex for public services. The buildings for public services, designed by different architects, are clustered around the circular armature which houses galleries, restaurants and allows for circulation around a ceremonial plaza. The individual buildings can be enhanced by form and materials appropriate to the program and symbolic role of each. This offers citizens more opportunities to orient themselves and leads to a better understanding of the services as a working complex. (*Drawings by Herb Greene.*)

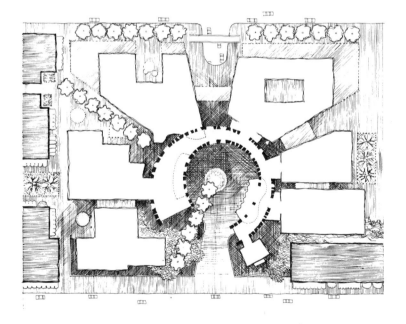

bolizing, not government or commerce but rather a community of people, a centuries-long stream of images contributed by both architects and the community. Public architecture will come to symbolize people-working-together, their creative talents producing visible evidence of their group existence. Millions of citizens are already creating crafts and arts in scattered places. Yet architecture in our time has not given them the opportunity to assemble even a fraction of their work as an intrinsic element of a building on a scale, accumulated, complex and continuing enough to visibly say, "this is the work of the public."

We need mechanisms to encourage the development and expression of the public. There has been a growing imbalance emphasizing the values of the private. Part of the reason cities are in decline is because of protectionism favored by private individuals and interest groups. In an analysis of how our inward turning culture has displaced public culture, Richard Sennett shows how current attitudes and prerogatives of privacy retard political and social development. He traces the growth of a narcissistic urge to view the world as self image and makes an important distinction between the energies of narcissism and the energies of play. During play children develop the power to be sociable and to be concerned with the quality of expression at the same time. Sennett attributes the current dominance of narcissism to the fact that there are few adult settings in which a nuance of risk, frustration and gratification can be found. Play teaches that immedi-

ate gratification can be suspended and replaced by interest in the content of rules: to objectify action, to put it at a distance and change it. Sennett views play as the energy of public expression—a situation where something more than gratification governs the players' acts, where we take risks in hope of finding a new pattern. An armature way of building with its requirements of participation and mix of aesthetic and social goals offers adult settings for play. By involving heterogeneous cross sections of the public in an on-going, patently self-transcending program that would touch peoples' lives and environment, at both neighborhood and city scales, architectural armatures could be a catalyst in forming a new expression of the public.

Rather than symbols of society as governors and governed, a public armature encrusted with the work of the many, willingly contributed, would project the image of a society of co-builders and the reality of co-decision makers. Hannah Arendt says in her book *The Human Condition*, "The public realm, as the common world, gathers us together and yet prevents our falling over each other, so to speak. What makes mass society so difficult to bear is not the number of people involved, or at least not primarily, but the fact that the world between them has lost its power to gather them together, to relate and to separate them." An armature with all its opportunities for citizens to participate is a way that architecture can become the world between us, both relating large numbers of people to each other in a constructive manner

and at the same time allowing each to be an individual.

An armature is intended as a summing-up. It answers the need to see ourselves as part of a whole. The scale of an armature which may not be large in bulk must be in tune with the larger social entity that encompasses the common image of its participating group. If this be an urban neighborhood, a suburban development, or a rural village, then the image of the whole may be particular, specific, local, ethnic, neighborly. Where participants are drawn from a city or region, the armature will encompass images at a larger scale with references that have meanings in common to more people, and at the national or even world scale an armature may seek cues that cut across all state or local boundaries and stress images that call to mind our common humanity. While including specific local references in armatures of any scale, even in the smallest, it will be possible and desirable to include references to the universal. The architect will sense appropriate images and scale for an armature framework in relation to its potential additions and encrustations of people's work so that the frame inspires metaphors that support without overwhelming the parts, and together they speak of an entire community whether the numbers be small or large. The human mind with its ability to make new meaning from new combinations of old images will, I believe, see an armature as a positive symbol of a pluralist society. With potential for democratic content, sociable gatherings and civic celebrations, a long-lasting armature at the city's core could revitalize individual participation in the public realm.

Natural Phenomena as Source of Powerful Images

When I say we can return to nature for new symbolism, I am going beyond the eighteenth and nineteenth centuries' romantic rediscovery of nature and natural beauty, drawing instead on twentieth century concepts that derive from the natural sciences.

The transformation of the material of the Earth's crust—fossils, vegetation, sediments, and magma—are taken as the basis for an armature metaphor, a building that does not merely sit on the Earth but that seems to be derived from the Earth itself. I see the armature as a kind of underlayerment symbolic of the earth as a background from which functional or fanciful forms, fragments of historic styles and contemporary additions can be seen to emerge as if from more primordial elements.

Properties most amenable to symbolic reconstitution are signs of stability, mass and erosion and the evidence of great age as seen in layers of rock and sediments; transformations from seas to solids; bands of fossils; and human settlements as unearthed by archeologists. Paralleling nature, forms and textures of the armature refer to the dense and the diaphanous, growth and decay, stability and change. I am seeking an expressive form in which the evolutionary process and the phenomenal properties of Earth will be seen as a context for an evolving cosmology.

In addition the ecological relationship between mankind and other living creatures can, I believe, inspire images to express our understanding that there are complex systems of living things on land, sea and in the sky, including the human species, that are interdependent for survival. Our present difficulties in grasping an ecological cosmology are frustrating because our Judeo-Christian tradition has been interpreted to mean that man is master of na-

ture, a concept now being reoriented through science to locate humankind in an interdependent position as *part* of nature. Working within an economic system that still perpetuates hierarchal concepts and expresses them architecturally in corporate high-rises and bank towers, I am asking the architect to turn for new inspiration to an ecological concept. Out of this century's environmental urgencies has come a new realization: that we need to give the natural world great care if we ourselves expect to breathe, eat and flourish. This care calls for changes in our way of thinking, our style of living and building. A more complex, ecologically responsive system of design and building can begin to make immediate and diverse contributions without waiting for some ideal society to come about.

As I see it, affluent societies are not likely to dramatically reverse their course and return voluntarily to simpler, less wasteful living in the immediate future, but it is not beyond possibility that we may soon come to a time of restricted resources or create major ecological disasters which could, if we survive, change our course. Nevertheless, understanding and change can be hastened; images and symbols can help us visualize a new direction. I think a combination of vision and practicality expressed in architecture can help set us on a

Stratified sedimentary rocks, thrust up from an ancient ocean floor, are revealed by river erosion in the palisades of the Kentucky River. (*Photo by Nanine Hilliard Greene.*)

46

Armature based on landform metaphors of the geological structure of the earth's crust, archeological layers of civilization, and organic life. A streaming continuum of time is implied. The public armature, a three-story interface with streets bounding an urban block, is a dark mass covered with reliefs, accessible to pedestrians on one side and vehicles and pedestrians on the other. The street face is conceived as a mosaic tapestry never to be completed. Openings are for a variety of stores and offices at street level. Additional light streams in from wells through the roof. The glassy building above the armature contains residences and offices developed by the private sector, and utilizes the principle of a continuous "sun porch," two meters deep and functioning as a heat trap or insulating buffer. (*Drawing by Herb Greene.*)

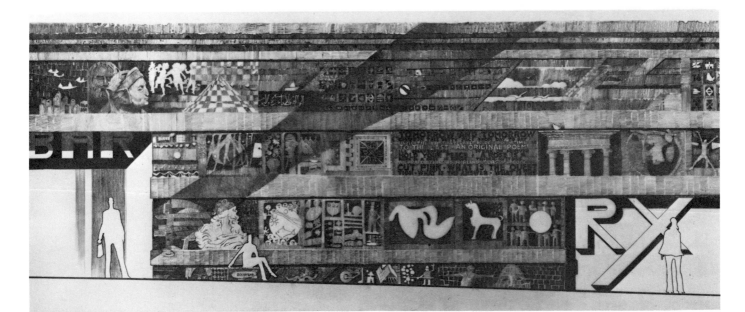

Closeup of an armature wall. Architect and artist facilitators coordinate the works of citizens and artists. The individuality of each piece is protected and adds meaning to a larger public frame. The wall is of load-bearing masonry with exposed structural lintels which support future openings. Designs made of ceramics, glass, concrete, metals and other materials are applied as surfaces between lintels. After designated periods, new designs are made to replace the old. (*Drawing by Herb Greene.*)

47

course in which we exist functionally and symbolically in a more ecological relationship to our planet, our cities and to each other.

It is also possible that we may continue to build irresponsible, energy-wasteful structures and camouflage them under superficially "ecological" shapes and surfaces. By ecological I mean that a building must take into account the conservation of world-wide resources: the materials used, the total energy consumed in the building process as well as the costs of operation. When I urge the use of regional materials it is not for aesthetic reasons alone but to save energy consumed by transportation. A long-lasting armature also intends to make maximum use of the materials and energy it does consume. Its basic frame lasts for centuries. Its ornamented surfaces are built to last and to be recycled. The armature becomes a substantial frame for short-lived additions that can employ lightweight materials which do not require excessive energy or the consumption of non-re-newable resources. I would also extend the meaning of ecological to include a wide range of local creative work through which human energy and social diversity can be utilized in building and ornamenting our environment. A system of building that fosters collaboration and participation by many citizens will, I believe, become a symbol of interdependence that represents our understanding of both nature and human society and our ethical responsibilities to each. The basis for a new design symbolism is latent in this enlarged ecological awareness.

We have arrived at a time when expensive but impermanent buildings are no longer feasible. A building that conserves all these energies in the long run and reveals this visibly is more than an expedient way to save money. It is a positive symbol of a caring attitude toward the earth's resources and of a willingness to change our way of building so we begin to live in reality.

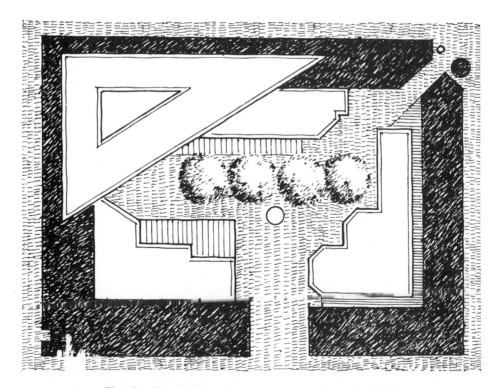

Plan for the armature with landform metaphors showing private additions, in white. The dark shaded areas indicate the long lived elements. (*Drawing by Herb Greene.*)

4 Tragedy and Humor as Polarities in Armatures

All around me the armature projects a sense of timelessness and awe. Suddenly across an electronic signboard built into the encrusted facing flies Snoopy in his Sopwith Camel.

BY tragedy in architecture I mean the need to convey a sense of destiny and the inevitable. The tragic poet implies that there are unchanging moral or natural laws behind the activities of humankind and nature. Too, tragedy always includes references to the past. Its concern is with timelessness. It is an emotional state dealing with values and historical associations. In the expressive forms of an armature I intend the larger whole to be in the tragic mode. By this I intend a sense of order implying a grand inevitability that is the nature of the universe and of life itself.

Tragedy, a dominant theme in literature, theater and dance, has been conveyed with deep emotion in painting, sculpture and music. At times architecture has included expressions of tragedy as in the foreboding pyramids of Mayan temples or in the solemnity and pathos of Michelangelo's sculpted moldings for St. Peter's. However, in much contemporary architecture, tragedy is missing. Function, technology, behaviorist planning and more recently

stylistic mannerism are the dominant concerns. Most architecture growing out of expedient commercialism lacks any vital sense of history and therefore can in no way lend itself to the treatment of profound tragedy. This sense of tragedy, so strongly evident in the dynamic and growth-inspired architecture of Frank Lloyd Wright and the austere simplifications of Mies Van Der Rohe, is now in disrepute. In its place is an amoral attitude and preferences that reflect mere automatism and the expedient aspects of life. It is justifiable to question recent monumental architecture which for the most part is not tragic but simply overwhelmingly large, "heroic" and authoritarian. I intend quite different meanings for an armature. To express tragedy, images of the historic continuum, of the emotions of a participating public and of an ecological relationship between humankind and nature may at times call for some degree of size as a necessary component but the monumentality required for the tragic mode in armatures excludes the glorification of private enterprise, governmental authority or heroic egos.

Monumentality is a function of scale relationships and content more than bulk. Even the small houses of Frank Lloyd Wright often pro-

49

A Sullivan design on the wall of a hospital. Sullivan, Gaudi, and Wright, architects of the organic tradition, often aspired to create art symbols stemming from cosmic order. Ferrero's magnification of a Louis Sullivan design, strives for a sense of cosmic power mingled with notions of joy and regeneration. It is conceived as a labor-intensive exercise in mold making and concrete casting. The original design, a pencil drawing less than 18" high, is enlarged to three-story height, to become textural relief for a blank surface and to provide a blossoming plant-like form as a sym-

bol of vital energy, and to express awe and wonder at the life process.

The eighteenth century English essayist Joseph Addison attributed aesthetic emotion to large size. Institutional authority and other negative connotations can also be read into great size. However, in this image the joyous tree occurs in a field with cues like promenades for sun, air and exercise, formed by small trees and trellises; and many windows which suggest a variety of human needs; altogether an expression of humanist themes. (*Drawing by Harvey Ferrero, Architect.*)

ject a sense of monumentality by their accumulative form and powerful proportions. At the same time they have human scale, human control, warmth and accommodation. The monumentality of an armature is not that of an architect's ego, identified with his own creation (a criticism sometimes leveled at Wright), nor the overpowering stance equated with institutional authority. Armatures allow a dialogue among individuals of a democratic society and the expression of the inevitable patterns of time, culture and natural forces from which we have evolved. These symbols, in order to convey the tragic sense, call for appropriate degrees of monumentality.

Tragedy in architecture will bring together cues that mingle feelings of reverence, wonder, awe, even dread, inspired by the majestic and sublime. The challenge is to structure an appropriate set of architectural cues and contexts to evoke a genuinely deep-felt sense of the tragic. Among the design aims for an armature, especially a large urban armature, are a concentration of cues suggesting mass, power, transformation, complexity and wonder that enable us to recover the emotion of awe. The incorporation of thousands of individual expressive acts into surfaces and pavements will enrich and humanize an armature making it a place to pay respects to preceding generations. This creates a potential for reverie, sanctity and the sense of the inevitable.

Just as the builders of cathedrals found the tragic mode in religious sources, I am asking the architect to seek the tragic in other realities of the twentieth century. I am equating tragic with profound positive inevitabilities—our new understanding of space and time and of our mandatory coexistence with our fellow human beings and nature. I have often felt that the roots of tragedy, so extensive in their hold on human experience, are perhaps ultimate contexts by which architecture is evaluated in terms of feelings. We praise architecture out of proportion to its functional success when we recognize in it the appropriate embodiment of tragic values.

Although its opposite emotion, humor, is even less common in architecture, examples of built fantasy show that the comic spirit can be expressed in buildings. Public armatures are intended to encompass expressions of these two ageless barometers of human experience. By their very nature armatures added to and worked on by many architects and citizens over centuries offer unique opportunities to convey the sense of timeless order which is essential for tragedy and at the same time, reflect dissatisfaction with that order, the element essential for humor.

As tragedy in the world is best realized by contrasting grand regularities against capricious events, the historic order of the armature will act as a foil for the irreverent and unforeseen acts of citizen artists. Because the armature is a sculpture never to be finished, and because its users enjoy freedom to leave their mark on the built environment, a situation usually thwarted by present-day institutions, it is hoped an armature will reflect the deepest feelings which humankind can express. These will inevitably be grounded in forms of tragedy and released in comic intrusions.

Comedy reveals our situation in ways that tragedy cannot. Today our confusion over authoritarian governments, technological threats, ecological dilemmas, conflicts within our psychic nature, and our eroding beliefs in long-established institutions has produced a sense of the absurd that has become the background for much of life itself. Modern humankind lives each day with tragic-comic-absurd views of life that do not exclude each other and which are intertwined and must, I believe, be incor-

porated into the buildings that surround us.

If architecture can evoke the sense of tragedy then humor in the built environment is its natural polarity. If the grand metaphors of the basic structures are tragic, meaning they suggest ideal order and the perfect, then the compromise between the ideal order and the imperfect actual order is cause for the comedic. Making buildings in anticipation of the clash between the inevitable order requisite for tragedy and the humor that will occur in a collage of people's crafts, art and improvisitions presents possibilities for creating a new level of meaning. An armature comprised of original works inevitably contradicting the established state of things, will act as an antidote to the anomie of an institutionalized and mass produced environment. The ancients appended grotesques and gorgons to buildings to cause the adversary to laugh and thus disarm him. In an armature this superstition gives way to the use of humor to protect ourselves from ourselves.

Admittedly architecture, as we have thought of it in the past, is a difficult medium for the expression of humor. A humorous gesture is dulled by repetition, and buildings, being relatively permanent tend, like an old joke, to be "told" over and over again. On an armature the changing collage of people's art will enliven the building, offering contrapuntal jibes at the long lasting, tragic order implied by the basic monumental frame. As the years pass, I can imagine the impact of constantly changing work added to, piece-by-piece, or taken away and replaced by new generations creating surprise, shock, delight and irony.

Humor as Fresh Experience

In an architecture of collage and pluralist participation, the value of humor and its role in human life will become central themes because collage with its spontaneously contradictory combinations is a technique that is unavoidably an instrument of humor. Above all other causes, humor stems from a spirit of play and discovery akin to art. The basic action of humor is play, and the linking of habitually mismatched but self-consistent ideas, so typical of humor, is the structural key to the creative process. The desire to play, the welcomed outlets for personal or group creativity and the resulting humor will fulfill deep-seated needs in human beings.

In a yearning for play and fantasy, we have seen the appearance of the hand-built houses of the 1960's and '70's, small whimsical buildings that incorporate found materials in imaginative combinations. The work of individuals, these dwellings are usually hidden in out-of-the-way places. An armature can bring the imagination and skills of these builders to the public realm (if they wish to come), enriching the city's walls and pavings, creating spaces and shapes full of texture, color, excitement and whimsy. Well done fantasy such as Simon Rodia's Watts Towers, Clarence Schmidt's many-windowed castle and Cheval's Le Palais Ideal receive continuing attention and publicity, I believe, because they touch deeply so many people.

The interest and delight we take in fantasies can also represent the deepest kind of criticism. By focusing our attention on that which is unfamiliar and strange we enjoy an imaginative respite from the safe playing limits and logic that govern our action in what we suppose to be the actual world. Thus humor and fantasy play important roles as statements of ideals.

A public armature presents new opportunities for fantasy because the responsibility for image making lies not only with one individual architect or one builder but with a group of citizens who need not be conservative. Individuals and institutions may enjoy expressing themselves but usually refrain from building anything too subject to criticism. Participants in the public realm of the armature will not only be free to delve into the world of imagination but in a sense will be obligated to do so. Since individual risk will be lessened and since the task of the armature is to encourage imagination, release from social pressures to conform and the desire to get into the spirit of the work with one's peers can produce potent results.

Architecture has an age-old tradition of standing as a symbol of the deepest and most serious manifestation of institutions and of the self. We have not been able to treat these symbols with levity. It is like injecting humor into theology: it destroys the rigor and sanctity on which our institutions depend. All institutions want to keep the status quo, which laughter threatens. While some should be overthrown, most need reforming and constant changing. Thus, a healthy tradition of humor is a prerequisite for healthy institutions. If we can reach a level of maturity that accepts and integrates criticism of our institutions by realizing we can and must laugh at their inevitable incongruities and inequities, we could see that the comic is the ultimate evolutionary reformer and civilizer.

In a pluralist society in which a variety of ethnic and interest groups are vying for identity and influence, the expression of controversial issues can be expected. Humor can be the deepest expression of controversy. On the armature the use of humor is not intended to avoid conflict but to allow us to convert hostility and direct it while at the same time permitting its expression. I envision the armature as a vehicle that promotes a deeply comic intention: the willingness to criticize the status quo for what is limited about it in the hope of effecting a better condition.

The armature will reserve areas for overt social criticism. These can range from school children's pleas for environmental protection to the equivalents of the high art caricatures of Daumier and the Rabelaisian work of Hogarth. Decisions for selecting pieces to be incorporated or removed will fall on a group representing all walks of life in the neighborhood or urban center. As our society broadens its tolerance for discord and indeterminacy and becomes cognizant that much of art that wins our highest respect is ambiguous and capable of multiple readings, we will also see that buildings and pieces of their ornament can tell us what is valued even if they cannot set things right.

Though we may laugh with and at others, we all know that the human animal does not like to be laughed at and has a hard time laughing at him or herself. Mechanisms for this behavior have developed over our evolutionary past and are so ingrained in us and in our institutions that a successful application of humor to architecture will require an accepted rationalization of its benefits to a democratic society and will

San Francisco's City-County building modeled in bread dough and cast in bronze for Ruth Asawa's fountain on the steps of the Hyatt House Hotel. Are those eagle wings a jibe at federal revenue sharing? (*Photo by Laurence Cuneo*)

call for strategies that protect the ego against unnecessary wounds. There is some evidence that the U.S. and England are beginning to accept more humor and satire in the public built environment. In recent years large humorous wall murals have become the civic-thing-to-do, although some of them strike me as being unnecessarily obtrusive. In a few cities, political and ethnic murals have appeared showing that the public, or at least certain neighborhoods, can tolerate controversial comment. And on the highways, bumper stickers with their political and religious messages attest to the individual's need to express opinions publicly. An armature can dignify comments like these by setting them in an aesthetic and philosophic context. While most of us are offended by unwanted graffiti, specific features of an armature will allow for timely expressions and quick erasures. We can allow communication of the most contemporaneous fashions and interests and of even the hottest issues without recourse to the permanence of concrete and steel. While some

graffiti has iconic and decorative value, its main role is to let off steam. On an armature I wouldn't be surprised to see lampoons of the armatures themselves with all their cosmic posturing!

A wall in Philadelphia was intentionally painted white, providing a fresh surface for new spray paintings, new comments and a place for neighborhood drawings. (*Photo by Nanine Hilliard Greene.*)

Cartoon by Forrest Wilson.

can't be sure if the humor is intended or not, as in the lobby of the New York State Theater in Lincoln Center where Philip Johnson has two Nadelman figures blown up and set at either end. They look down smugly at everyone, like culture mavens about to donate or refuse a grant to the arts. Since exaggeration from the norm often strikes us as funny, Johnson's blow-ups are susceptible to humorous readings. Another humorous strategy that can be built into an armature will be for solemn buildings to become amusing through interaction with human beings. Even ornamented lintels and cartouches can transform a window into a stage set capable of recurring humor. I can imagine this kind of fun consciously planned for: openings that become portrait frames; a wall with rows of heads atop; beasts with people sitting on them, and so on. We might take clues from (but not imitate) the tacky inventions of restaurants whose patrons, looking for amusement, eat out in fake cabooses, elevators, life boats—anything to get away from the boredom of simplistic settings.

A humorous setting is made by the architects Venturi, Rauch and Brown in the Guild House apartments in Philadelphia by placing dead center of the front door an oversized one story circular column sheathed in marble. In the context of flat walls, low-scale entry doors and oversized name plate, the column is an unexpected yet familiar sign of wealth and glory from the days of cheap labor, big budgets and monumental entrances. Its fat grandeur arouses expectations soon dissipated by collision with the thin and boxy concrete balconies of utilitarian construction. The column reminds us that people conventionally enjoy walking into an entrance made important. But here they have to contend with the icon of pomp as if it were an obstacle, dodging its ponderous form on their way through the door. I suggest that the architects would not have used such a device in the doorway of a rich and prominent client, and that a welcoming entrance, rather than a possibly satiric one, would have been more appropriate for an apartment for the elderly. Nonetheless, with their incongruous column, Venturi, Rauch and Brown have revived humor as a source of serious architectural imagery.

Strong social factors will, of course, play a role in defining what is permissible in the expression of comedy. Given the context of an armature built by citizens, for use by citizens and controlled by citizens in a social milieu that is gradually increasing its tolerance, we can expect a high level of responsibility and humor.

There are, of course, some examples of humor in present day architecture from Hansel and Gretel suburban houses to pompous neoclassic buildings. Some is intentional (hot dog stands in hot-dog-shaped buildings, for example), much of it is unintentional and most of it is camp and kitsch. Some is ambiguous: one

Guild House, Philadelphia, Pennsylvania. Robert Venturi, architect. (*Photo by Bob Vuyosevich*)

I can envision a wealth of similar but more imaginative opportunities designed into an armature. There could be mini-piazzas, spatial theaters with optical illusions and humorously distorted props simulating the symbolically alienating but nonetheless warmly colored and affecting surrealistic paintings of the early DeChirico. Or steps like the entrance to the New York Public Library where guardian lions are placed so that people can stand between sculpted paws. In an overtly comic gesture the lions might be asleep, their tails to be twisted by children. Accommodating the human form, our lions would make an interlude of play and seats for adults. They also remind us that we, not they, must guard our valued institutions.

Moore's stage set fountain and piazza is intended as a catalyst for renewal in an Italian neighborhood. The use of painted stucco, of columns of water from shower heads, and of neoclassic moldings add whimsy but, as in the case of Venturi's fat column, raise questions of whether the humor is at the expense of a relatively powerless or unsophisticated user-client—a neighborhood, an ethnic or age group—that may not be able to judge ahead of time the degree to which they or their position in the community is being satirized.

Place D'Italia, New Orleans, Louisiana. Charles Moore, Architect. (*Photo by Nanine Hilliard Greene.*)

55

According to the designer, this out-of-scale back wall of the Louden Nelson Community Center, Santa Cruz, California, has been given "goodness of fit" by a mural, a colorful reminder of a street with painted neighbors on painted balconies watching the scene below. Jeff Oberdorfer, architect-facilitator, says, "People find the mural emotionally appealing because it suits the site so well." The over-scaled painted residents express desired sociability and provide humorous protest against a blank façade. (*Photos by Jeff Oberdorfer.*)

Prairie House, Norman, Oklahoma. Herb Greene, architect. As sculpture on the plains of Oklahoma, this house uses images of anthropomorphism and creaturehood as the element of shock. The aim is to introduce a reference frame of feeling usually reserved for sentient creatures. Pathos, vulnerability and pain are juxtaposed with the more familiar house-meanings of sheltering, protection and comfort. (*Photo by Bob Bowlby.*)

The Shock of Incongruity

The use of incongruity to shock the viewer into seeing latent or unsuspected meaning between consistent but incompatible ideas is an artistic tool to create humor. Allegra Stewart writing on the use of this device in the work of Gertrude Stein describes how incongruities may stem from the artist's unconscious guidance. The conscious mind is quick to grasp the intention of the incongruous incident and display it, fait accompli, in an image or build on it with additional references. She calls it the element of shock or the displacement of accent which attracts attention and causes pleasure. It is an element that is not at first glance formally unified with the structure. It exerts a kind of pressure, therefore, to force analysis to another level.

What is considered comical in primitive societies is strikingly similar to what we find humorous, a parallel that confirms the elemental nature of humor. However, it is the more primitive societies that continue to maintain expressions of the ambivalent feelings between the sacred and profane. The Hopi have rites in which customs, objects and beliefs, normally regarded with the greatest reverence and respect, are treated with ceremonial ridicule. Even the medieval church knew how salutary is the comic rite of unmasking, and monks used to appoint one of their number to chant the liturgy of folly. An ass was worshipped and the Mass parodied.

If traditions of humor in architecture do develop, one result may be that the protracted influence of clichés derived from great architects will be diminished. For hero worship is incompatible with humor. There may be fewer mediocre and inappropriate copies, not so much because of the lack of temptation by disciples and casual rip-off artists, but because the public will have recourse to a mode of criticism and because the armature concept represents a self-criticizing advance into new forms of expression.

Since most architecture has traditionally avoided the conscious application of humor, why do we seek to alter that tradition at a time when most clients want buildings to be uncontroversial and quickly amortized? First, the rapid growth of mass production, as we have noted, has produced an often boring and alienating environment badly in need of mitigating design strategies. Secondly, the extensive growth of middle-class values in the nineteenth and twentieth centuries that led to a prosaic attitude toward life, has been challenged by the recent generation which has tried to loosen this posture by encouraging dissent and by adopting colorful, even poetic, individualization in dress, decoration, food, and houses. I believe it is time for architects to recognize that a change in the public's aesthetic values has taken place. A healthy tradition of humor can add a dimension to architecture that will touch everyone.

The Anti-Tragic

Some "humor" arising from the anti-heroic movement in architecture is distinctly anti-tragic and even anti-moral. I believe it is worth a brief comment to distinguish this kind of humor from that intended by armatures.

Since the sixties architects have reacted against prevailing doctrines of heroic architecture. They have challenged minimalist purity, technocratic design controls and messianic social claims. Influenced by absurd theater and pop painters some champion wit and irony gained by mixing popular, consumer culture with the architectural traditions of high culture. They argue for the acceptance of "people's" taste as evidenced by the commercial roadside strip culminating in the plethora of signs, drive-ins and casinos of Las Vegas where a variety of shapes, messages and chance juxtapositions supposedly produce humor and vitality. While this acceptance appears to support a democractic attitude, the humor in the signs is undermined by their fundamental aim: to sell. This kind of humor is cheapened because there is no tragic mode present. The products of expedient commercialism lack a sense of history requisite to tragedy. To equate an A & P parking lot with a European parterre, and to describe the sign on Caesar's Palace at Las Vegas, a 100% kitsch plastic and plaster construction, as being more Etruscan than Roman (as if it made any difference) is to devalue history. One sees analogies, of course, but the point is that hotel signs and supermarket parking lots are dictated only by advertising and commercial interests. Historic associations, expressions of sacredness, the object's place in a cosmology, any cultural substance, morality or even joy cannot be found.

To be comedic, humor must be set against the tragic backdrop. Tragedy calls for aspiration, heroism, or other components of the "noble" in dealing with inevitable order. Perhaps many architects feel that the present situation of humankind with its mass cultures, bureaucracies and nuclear threats is such that nobility of purpose in the face of these overwhelming absurdities is either false or futile. The uncertainty hypothesis of science can be interpreted to undermine the sense of human beings in control of their destiny. Once we pinned our hopes on the aesthetic and social visions of geniuses such as Wright and Le Corbusier but have found these to be utopian, unworkable and authoritarian. Thus acceptance of commercialism or "things as they are" seems to some as both realistic and democratic. Further, the commercial milieu is sometimes interpreted as an outcome of Western tradition produced by the remorseless workings of inevitable destiny. Whitehead describes this attitude as exemplified by scientists who unconsciously accept their scientific findings as decrees of fate under the cultural influence of Greek tragedy. If we do the same, then it is a contradiction to accept strip development as fate while denying the tragic view. To accept the landscape of the automobile, created by expedient use of that machine which produces banal urban forms and drains resources at unconscionable rates (in the U.S. the auto pre-empts over 60% of urban land) is more a product of human shortsightedness than either pragmatism or fate. Nor is the argument that ordinary people *like* the resulting strip development a satisfactory recommendation. Current conceptions of free enterprise and the momentum of business requirements do not nourish alternatives—so the "common people" know no other possibility.

Thus a design strategy accepting "things as they are" becomes a commentary on manners that does not disturb anything fundamental to the economic, social or building systems which produce "things as they are." I see the prevailing system as trivializing the creative act of the individual in relation to the built environment. An armature philosophy of design intends to counteract the trend that glorifies commercial culture and hopes to reestablish and intensify the timeless dialogue between evidence of tragic themes and the comedic intrusion. Humor in architecture will then have a moral basis and expressions of the tragic will give people opportunity to reveal their deepest values.

A vehicle for public comedy in the built environment will likely foster not only the arts of humor and satire but will bring us together in convivial groups with shared appreciation for humorous elements discovered by others. As everyone knows we laugh far more easily in a group than alone, and that behavior related to humor crops up in most social encounters. I have been told that experiments indicate humor-related response to be ten times more prevalent than any other kind of emotional behavior.

If we can encourage expressions of humor in environmental settings we will meet emotional needs which have been overlooked in contemporary architecture. In addition to reinforcing the powerful image of a public place for coming together, an armature that includes humor will symbolize an ever-changing dialogue between the tragic and comic aspects of life.

Part Two / PRIVATE VISIONS: CITIZENS' ART AND CRAFTSMANSHIP

5 Creative Inconvenience

Jamie and Beth led me into their living room. Jamie's fingers follow the valleys of mortar joints between handmade bricks as he tells me he and Beth have bought this forty-year-old house attached to the two-hundred-year-old neighborhood armature. The soft red bricks are warm as the sun shines through a skylight, its insulating shutters opened wide this bright April day. The house smells fresh and earthy from air that flows from the community greenhouse bordering the backyard court. We climb to the top of the three story stair tower, which they will open in summer for ventilation, and look out over the neighborhood. Heavy masonry walls and mosaic paving make a richly textured lattice infilled with houses, gardens, greenhouses and trees. I see a gamut of styles added within the armature frame—an airstream trailer connected to the masonry wall by a membrane structure, a geodesic dome rising above a courtyard wall, gabled roofed houses and earth sheltered houses and houses where users have salvaged a circular silo and an industrial container and converted these into livable additions, all held together by the visual and real strength of the masonry armature and the habitable spaces it affords. Jamie points out an earth sheltered space on a public green where neighbors can be seen working on a center for sharing tools and other resources. Beth asks me to come back next year, when they plan to open up an old door through the masonry and spread out into the adjoining court that's coming up for lease.

I am using the term "creative inconvenience," a phrase coined by architect Michael Alcorn, to describe the creativity that results when people are given opportunity to respond to a built environment they did not originally produce. The design response to existing buildings often results in the conflict and collision of old and new. This conflict, once accepted and resolved, can be described as the design energy of two or more interacting systems. If we conceive an existing building as a system which gives us a unique repository of information—its material, stylistic references, time frame and history—and if we imagine ourselves adding to it, expressing our own needs and tastes and then accept future additions by users yet unknown, we are admitting to a complex aesthetic and a program of uncertainty and indeterminacy.

Uncertainty and indeterminacy have come to play key roles in science and art. The more cumbersome disciplines of architecture and planning have been less susceptible to theories of indeterminacy but, as I indicate at the end of this chapter, several recent proposals em-

Each neighborhood street connects to a pedestrian path and green space linking between two hundred and six hundred houses. Along this route are bicycle and jogging paths, small restaurants, services, a gardeners' and farmers' market, and a selection of shops to add liveliness and amenities to the community. From end to end the green space is negotiable by a five to seven minute walk and connects elementary school, community and resource center, shopping, recreation, offices and other places of work. The boundary feature of the pedestrian path is the three-story armature with habitable space approximately forty feet deep. This space is part of the long-lived framework and can accommodate professional offices, commercial uses and housing. Shop front additions and one or two more stories can be added to the armature. Rear courtyards allow expansion and gardens. The arrangement is such that the individual or family has the option to alter and renew the house within the armature and courtyard. By adding rooms and making stylistic modifications, the individual creates a personal domain and expresses his or her sense of history and home.

High-rise dwellings located at the ends of the spine and living spaces above shops along the spine increase typical subdivision density of three or four units per acre to eight to twenty units per acre and open considerable community space for recreation and gardens not found in the usual subdivision.

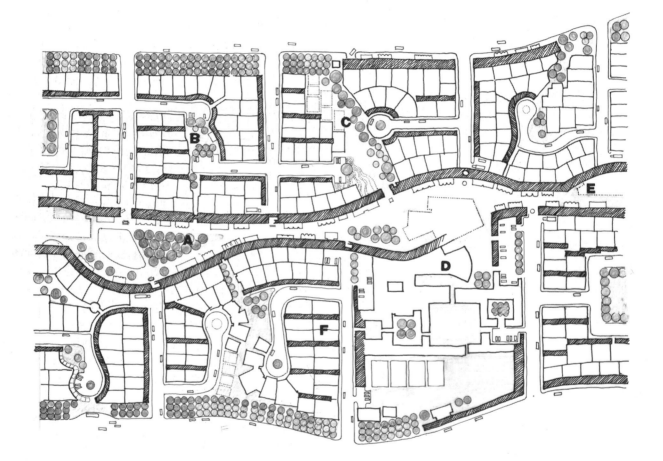

Plan of a Neighborhood Armature. Like a stabilized ruin conveniently awaiting appropriation and reuse, the habitable spaces of the armature (shaded) give shape to the community while allowing indeterminate additions and infill. Landscape, artfully and ecologically considered, is itself developed as an armature or an integral part of one. The architect will take advantage of natural features such as terrain, trees, plants, wind, water and sky because literally and symbolically these are deeply embedded in our biological and psychological being. Key to plan: (A) Pedestrian spine, water and gardens. (B) Neighborhood green space. (C) Neighborhood green space with gardens and orchards. (D) Elementary school, community center and recreation. (E) Space for major building additions. (F) Lots for individual courtyard houses. (*Drawing by Herb Greene.*)

ploy strategies of additions and unforeseen development. For armatures, indeterminacy is particularly apt, especially when an armature is intended for housing and gives form to an entire neighborhood. The mix of people that constitutes an ideal neighborhood with varied interests at different times of the day or year creates diverse activity that does not exist in places of work, schools, commercial areas and institutional buildings. The need for individuals and families to establish territory and personal expressions of home obviously calls for design strategies that provide aesthetic inspiration and practical utility while allowing

According to Drs. Jean Mayer and Johanna Dwyer, noted nutritionists, homegrown vegetables and fruits are annually valued at over $15 billion. Research indicates people garden in order to have better quality fruits and vegetables, to save money and for enjoyment. Trees and green areas are the settings preferred by 95% of Americans for their homes. Space for gardening and greenery will be an intrinsic part of a residential armature. (*Photo by Nanine Hilliard Greene.*)

Crossroads Community (The Farm), San Francisco, California. Unused land under a city freeway interchange has been transformed into a farm. Here urban children have the chance to raise animals and learn gardening. In and around an abandoned warehouse building, Bonnie Sherk, the artist who conceived and initiated the project, has mixed mirrors and maquettes, fantasy and reality, vegetables and animals in a combination of art and life. Youngsters and adults work together in a community vegetable garden and create theater in the "farm house gathering space." Bonnie Sherk sees The Farm as a place for social art, as a model of a microcosm of nature and as the beginning of a framework of open spaces that will connect neighborhoods, schools, parks in

the area. Already the City of San Francisco has purchased, at the urging of The Farm, five adjoining acres.

The Farm, in its unlikely spot, illustrates using a piece of the city as a found object in such a way that a novel sense-of-place is created. The underside of an expressway is certainly not an ideal starting point and yet the heavy piers and sheltering roadway have a mass and a degree of permanence that invite additions and ornament. The variety of activities that center around raising plants and animals in small urban spaces are similar to those intentionally designed into a neighborhood armature. (*Photo by Nanine Hilliard Greene.*)

flexibility in adapting space and opportunities for unforeseen creative expression. This is not to say that some existing models of housing have not allowed for these objectives but that we need new models in light of changing realities concerning economics, energy, natural resources and aesthetics with its current recognition of indeterminacy.

It is only recently that neighborhoods have been zoned homogeneously residential. This was possible only because mechanized transportation and cheap fuel substituted for walking to what had to be nearby work, shops, and schools. New low density sprawl in many U.S. subdivisions is producing high costs in terms of utilities, roads, and other services. I am hypothesizing a neighborhood in which a long-lasting armature frame with its additions will foster a complex mixture of housing, work places, educational and recreational oppor-

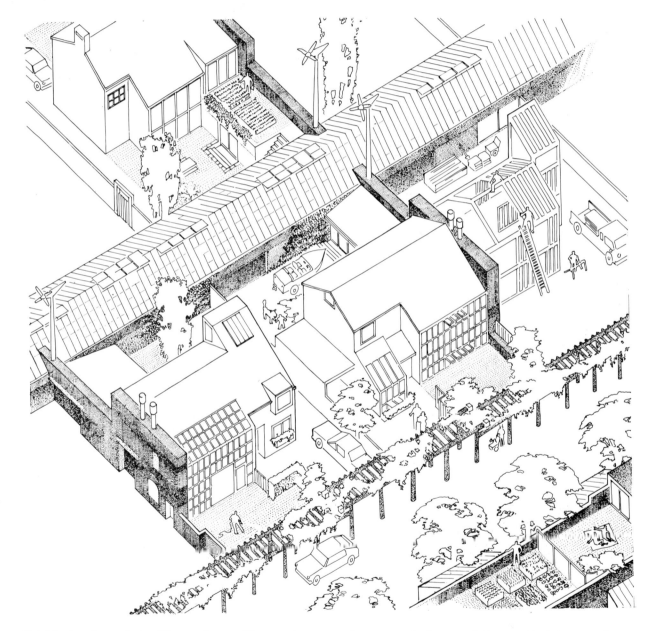

Neighborhood armature with greenhouse. The armature includes a thick-wall, masonry feature (shaded). Houses are shown with two-story porches with south exposure. A trellis over the sidewalk is maintained as a feature of the armature. It is low enough to permit solar access, while providing a prominent landscape feature in the neighborhood.

A permanent element of the armature is a continuous greenhouse which provides supplementary solar heat for adjoining houses. Part of a neighborhood network, the greenhouse can be used for winter produce and decorative plants and provides a source of work, income and common endeavor for the community. (*Drawing by Herb Greene.*)

tunities, as well as provide psychological benefits in terms of stability and the opportunity for creative work.

The solid yet unfinished characteristics of the neighborhood armature invite residents to build and renovate with a high degree of user autonomy. Habitable space within the thick-wall permanent frame reduces the size and cost of that other portion of each house provided by the user. Energy consumption for the isolated suburban house, exposed on all sides, is becoming unfeasible while workmanship on de-veloper-built houses grows more expensive and more careless. The neighborhood armature gives the homeowner incentives to invest individually and to contribute his or her own workmanship without perpetuating the single family house, townhouse or condominium as we now know them.

I have intentionally chosen an armature form that I believe suited to a middle class neighborhood in the United States because that is the setting with which I am most familiar.

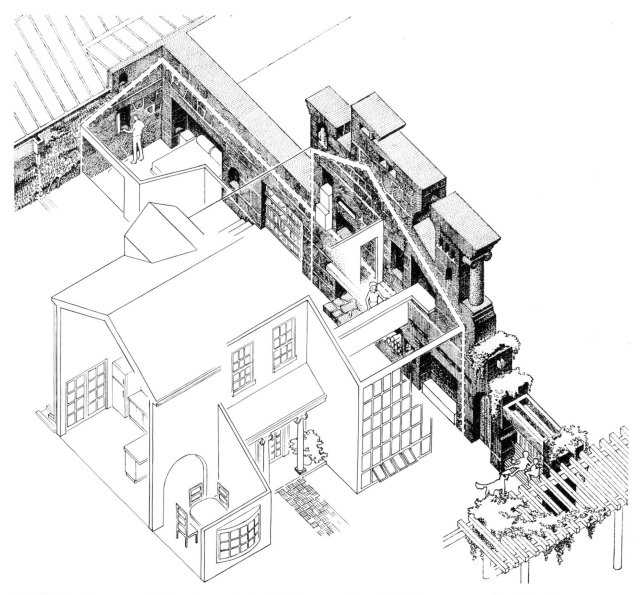

Neighborhood armature with housing attached. A thick-walled feature of crafted masonry becomes a stimulus for residents to respond with personal creativity. Beyond carrying utilities, providing a fire break between houses and making niches and hearths that encourage user adap-tations, it is built to suggest a ruin which allows us to compare the state of our present architecture with an imagined past. As well as permitting insets of personal ornament it also allows references to various cultural developments and historic periods. (*Drawing by Herb Greene.*)

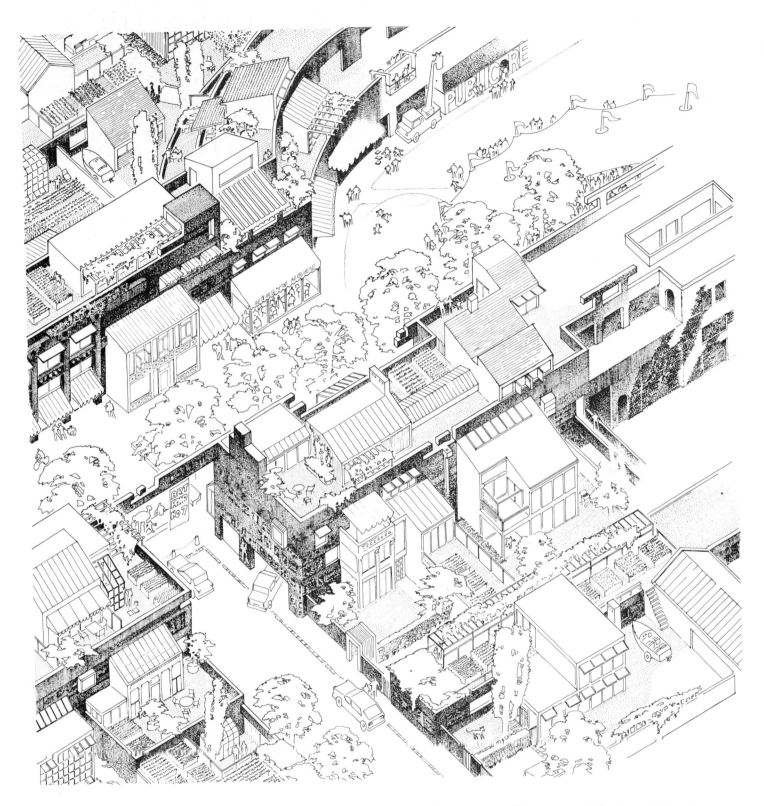

Neighborhood three-story armature with below-grade parking bounds the pedestrian spine, increasing density and creating shops and workplaces while allowing extensive additions. Shaded in a dot pattern, the armature suggests how ornamental features and allusions to historic styles and ruins could emerge. It also shows unfinished surfaces covered temporarily with vines. (*Drawing by Herb Greene.*)

Courtyard gate, Cranbrook, Michigan. Eliel Saarinen, architect. Saarinen has executed a pediment in which the design of small brick tiles is contrasted to normally scaled brick to evoke a Romanesque façade of much greater size. As a suggestion of an architectural evolution the past is brought to the present with seriousness and charm. This fascinating use of the miniature suggests possibilities for the armature wall. (*Photo by Ron Tilford.*)

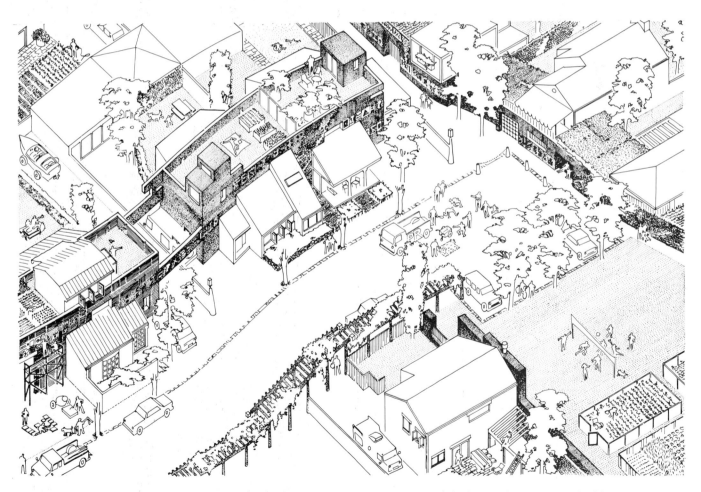

This neighborhood armature is an enclosed space of two and three stories (shaded), made of masonry planned so that users can adapt and add to the interior and exterior. Thick walls and earth on the roof provide insulating mass as well as crafted textures and substance that is usually beyond the reach of all but the wealthy. South-facing solar porches at the rear of the lots, and entrances and additions (unshaded) on the north, facing the street, show user determinations. Walls between lots and light standards (not shaded) could also be armature pieces. Garages, studios and small apartments at the rear of the lot can be user-determined. (*Drawing by Herb Greene.*)

Common open spaces are combined with long-lasting built elements to form a structuralized sculpture that includes dwelling space, recreation areas, streets and walkways, neighborhood greenhouses, gardens and orchards. To this will be attached privately built additions and courtyards. The aesthetic bias is to create an asymmetric and relaxed environment as opposed to a regimented and predictable one. Purposeful asymmetry, always difficult to achieve when based solely on visual grounds, will be accomplished through responses to solar orientation, a variety of lot sizes, house types as developed by residents, and various conditions of entrances, auto courts and mews. In cold climates lots will generally be arranged for maximum southern exposure which will program more variety into the neighborhood than does our usual orientation to the street.

By the use of models to be inspected before they build or alter their houses, residents might become aware of the following additional options:

Openings in permanent armature walls allow two or more lots to be combined or allow access between houses and shops. Larger lots can be divided into two.

Solar access: additions arranged so no courtyard is blocked from the sun by neighbors' buildings.

Stair towers to the level of the highest floor to act as breeze catchers and ventilators. The top floor of the tower may be a closed study or open observation deck with a windmill or solar water heater.

Work places may be incorporated in the armature of the house where they do not destroy privacy, quiet, and cleanliness.

Kitchen plans that allow a view to the front court and parking area or kitchen plans that look out on the rear courtyard or plans that do both, allowing residents surveillance of young children, visitors and the street or to have the privacy of their court and garden.

Courtyard walls have configurations which give structural stability, provide gates, niches and indentations and suggest accommodation for storage, planting and seating.

Movable canvas-and-pipe partitions on low walls separate courtyards to create visual privacy and diminish the sense of confinement.

Service access to the courtyard, garages and utility room.

Garage roof as open deck or closed-in extra room.

A neighborhood organized around a long-lived armature is intended to allow residents to take care of some of their own public services. As inflation causes the cost of street cleaning, trash collection and recycling, mail delivery, etc. to escalate, and as the increase in the size of urban populations produces large bureaucracies needed to provide these services, a neighborhood armature gives definition to a limited area in which services can be augmented by residents. An armature tries to recapture some of the qualities of the small town where people meet at the local post office to pick up mail and exchange news. The "creative inconvenience" intended by a residential armature is not only a built response to the physical frame but a social response in terms of increased self-sufficiency and in cooperative relationships between neighbors.

I am seeking to avoid the single age, single layer socioeconomic development that characterizes so many post-war suburbs, and to allow a variety of housing units so that the larger family, singles, and the elderly will be able to co-exist. By integrating a mix of work spaces, services, recreation, dwellings, commercial shops, community gardens and greenhouses, I hope to encourage relationships among people of many ages so a lively, secure, self-nourishing environment is created. Resurgent loyalty to identifiable neighborhoods is occurring across the nation and the rising price of gasoline is making us seek satisfactions at our own doorsteps. Recent growth of neighborhood associations, initially as defense against encroachment from highways, urban renewal, the destruction of historic buildings, etc., may now take on a new role: fulfilling the need for a neighborhood to

70

take care of its own services and to act as a social milieu and creative outlet for its residents. Planners, architects and builders will be looking for ways in which the physical design of new subdivisions can provide that degree of built-in "inconvenience" that allows residents to respond effectively and imaginatively. In older residential neighborhoods as well, I envision a service facility or service "gateway" utilizing or attaching to older buildings. Here, residents can collect mail, exchange tools, wash cars and recycle waste so the infernal garbage truck would not have to penetrate the early morning quiet of an enclave. The service building may also be a workshop for creative work. Perhaps a resident caretaker may be responsible for security and perform other service tasks in exchange for an apartment in the service gateway.

All features of the armature, including the permanent parts of each house, suggest a life span far beyond the length of use of any individual resident. These features are financed over long periods of time whereas those parts of the dwelling and courtyards infilled by residents are financed under current market practice.

Residents may modify their houses to fit the various stages of family life, for instance, renting out part when the children have left. One side of most lots is formed by a section of the long-lived framework that offers the user habitable space. It is a wall in some places and, in others, a heavy walled earth-on-roof structure that provides a cloistered retreat and a place for a roof garden. This habitable space is recessed two or three feet into the ground to increase the feeling of retreat and to lower the height of the exterior wall in the adjoining courtyard. Common walls between houses are of masonry to ensure acoustic privacy and still enable the nonbearing walls to be moved for the enlargement of one house into the other. In the light of current changes in family and social patterns and energy shortages, it seems desirable to develop a housing form where two, three or more groups can participate in cooperative living if they choose to.

In each neighborhood some version of the automobile is accepted. Perhaps an electric vehicle for local runs and a much smaller version of today's family car are reasonable conjectures. Eighty per cent of the units have parking courts or garages. These spaces can be utilized for workshops, storage or even additional living space but, I believe, are not to be dispensed with in any proposal that realistically faces Americans' present dependence on automobiles.

As the place where citizens potentially have control over a small area, I see a neighborhood armature offering self-transcendent work by creating jobs for the young and the retired, and by inviting personal expressions as ornament to the public environment. Ways in which the ingenuity of the individual or small group, working outside the mass production system, can find outlets for talents is a goal of a residential armature. Although there are similarities to projects intended for developing nations and the low income areas of cities, this neighborhood armature is not intended as architecture for the poor but architecture for the affluent-but-deprived.

Having a financial stake in the neighborhood, being continually involved in the design, and giving time and actions to realize some of its public as well as private physical form will add to a sense of identity with place. The opportunity to live in an aesthetically stimulating environment where others have lived before and will come after, and to modify that environment, is a visible way of participating in the historic process that creates a sense of stability. Adventure and wandering need not be obviated by goals for stability. As polarities of human drives, establishing place and mobility are complementary to each other. A physically beautiful neighborhood to which one has contributed in cooperation with others can be a stabilizing influence no matter what the term of residence. A continuing dialogue between the user and the richly symbolic framework will initiate individual creativity in both the private and community realms. In a society that has let excess and waste degrade the quality of life, an armature framework that allows for sizeable remodelings and replacement of worn out parts without destroying the structure makes real and ethical the conservation of resources.

Perez de Arce subjects some of Chandigarh's buildings, situated around open plazas and broad avenues, to revisionist planning by proposing an infill of structures to create habitable space and useful streets. Here Le Corbusier's Secretariat (center, rear) becomes the focus for new buildings following his own modular building types. (Drawings by Rodrigo Perez de Arce.)

Intentional "creative inconvenience," that is, the framework that invites additions and alterations, is paralleled by our recent interest in retrofitted and recycled buildings and alerts us to architectural examples throughout history where one society has overlaid the architecture of another. Recently, out of the philosophy of participation and advocacy planning of the 1960's has come a realization that the architect alone cannot satisfactorily determine all aspects of a building.

This questioning of architecture as a completed form has stimulated proposals for additions even to Modern architecture. Rodrigo Perez de Arce advocates a program of urban transformation by additions. To substantiate his proposal he shows how past generations incorporated the building stock of previous times into their urban fabric. By using existing architecture the likelihood of ongoing use is established. Since additions are based on what already exists, their development is characterized by low cost in both social and material

terms. Since infill does not require compulsory migration, some degree of continuity of the normal rhythm of life can be maintained. He rightly maintains that because additive transformation is a sedimentary process, it insures a continuity in historical and spatial terms, and that continuity is further reinforced by successive generations and, through the congruence of many people, a town of great quality almost necessarily evolves. Perez de Arce's description of the advantages of such a program is consonant with the values of "creative inconvenience" inherent in armatures. As he illustrates, the procedures of additive transformation, gradual revision and infilling by which towns evolved in the past are valid for modern times as well.

Contemporary cities, whether designed or created by happenstance often have a poor, loose, mechanical and repetitive structure of spaces that produces a sterility almost nonexistent in pre-modern towns. The need to infill well and give diversity again to modern cities will call forth ingenuity to remedy past mistakes. In an armature way of building we expect infill as integral to the original concept, not only as a corrective measure. Both newly created cores that are designed to age and existing buildings that are incorporated into armatures are planned so that in most cases layers of adjoining space can accommodate additions and subtractions.

Christopher Alexander and colleagues have developed a strategy for town planning and architectural design which favors piecemeal additions. Alexander, experienced in psychology and systems analysis, proposes that users design buildings by employing patterns of planning and construction which have developed over centuries. He and his team have designed procedures for people to analyze their needs (which they know best) and to make their own design proposals. Administration and funding would facilitate small-scale additions and foster post-construction evaluation and admit correc-

tions. Modest financial commitments would implement small-scale additions rather than large programs. With this scheme, however, the architecture of additions does not insure spontaneous ideas or novel shifts in design because patterns would be selected by users from Alexander's lexicon of what he believes are proven solutions from uncoerced vernacular architecture. His rational predictability would seem to preclude contingency and chance, and the possibility of invention by a creative designer or user would seem to be minimized.

I emphasize again that I am not proposing a structureless method. I believe that invention and creativity are touched off by having to respond to a limiting situation. I have often found that students of architecture do better when asked to remodel or add to an existing building than when expected to design a completely new structure on an open site. They show more enthusiasm and their work tends to be more competent when they do not have to

Roman walls and gate in Perugia as the base for later additions. (*Photo by Bob Vuyosevich.*)

73

invent from scratch, the usual goal of pedagogy derived from a perception of the architect as generator of original forms. The implication is that more people, perhaps relieved of an unrealistic expectation that they demonstrate complete originality to create a new building, can respond to the tangible limitations and affective ambience that many existing buildings possess. In the housing armature, given forms and textures will intentionally be an "inconvenience" to untramelled freedom and will provide positive stimuli to which numerous people can respond in numerous ways. As the armature is developed over time and its dual purpose as anchor and catalyst is understood, its value as both neighorhood stabilizer and stimulus to creativity will likely increase.

Since I suggest that strategies and design goals for armatures will find support in contemporary science and art, a brief explanation will show the connection. Though some historically important artists and schools have worked as if science never existed, many striking correlations occur. For example, the heightened expression of light in the paintings of Vermeer appears in the seventeenth century at the time when science developed new optical tools, analyzed the spectrum and proposed new theories explaining the physical basis of light.

The twentieth century is witnessing a shift in aesthetic attitudes. Where assumptions once favored homogeneous form and concepts of structure that were thought to be universally applicable, we now increasingly seek open-ended systems and apply local and specific criteria in determining structure.

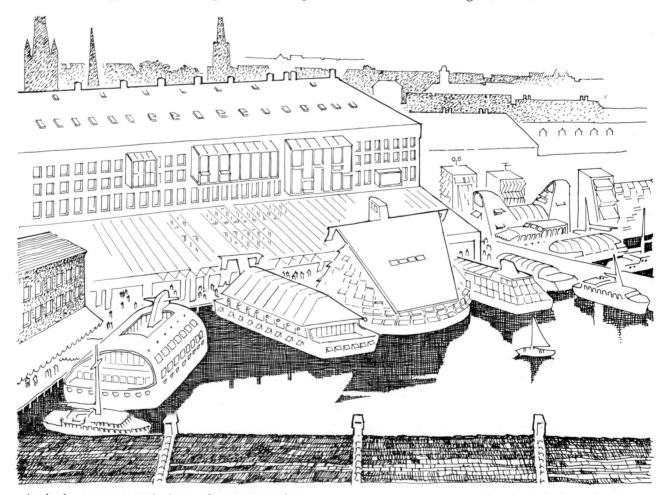

A wharf as an armature. A nineteenth century warehouse adapted for use as housing, offices and stores, and a glass-roofed quay-become-street is the armature. Additions are waterborne trade barges, offices, housing and other facilities. The barges with solar collectors can be rotated to gain maximum solar access. Utility hookups, perhaps under water, are provided to floating structures. A variety of building technologies and international styles will make a lively counterpoint to the historic armature. (*Drawing by Herb Greene.*)

The Theater of Marcellus in Rome, dedicated about 13 B. C. by Augustus Caesar, was added to in the Middle Ages and in the Renaissance to become housing and fortress for generations of Roman families. The preservation of ancient buildings in Rome has resulted in their absorption into the living city. The scale of the arches, their unexpected use as a base, and the curve of the wall, give invigorating contrasts to the housing additions. (*Drawing by Herb Greene. Adapted from the slide archives, College of Architecture. University of Kentucky.*)

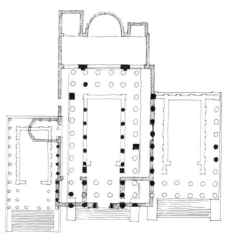

The Forum Holitorium, formerly the vegetable market of Rome, had three temples over which the church of S. Nicola in Carcere was erected, using walls and foundations of the earlier structures. Medieval tower, Renaissance front and Roman colonnades produce both harmonies and mismatches. (*Drawing by Herb Greene. Adapted from the slide archives, College of Architecture, University of Kentucky.*)

Forum Holitorium. The plan indicates three historical layers in the church we see today. (*Drawing by Herb Greene. Adapted from the slide archives, College of Architecture, University of Kentucky.*)

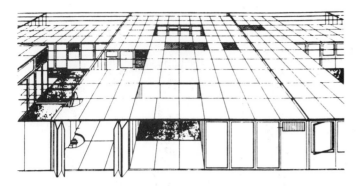

Willi Ramstein. Scholarship entry, Swiss Federal Commission for Art, 1963. This design, based on multiples of rectangular panels purporting flexibility, gives an indication of the mechanistic bias and penchant for predictability that was rampant in some design schools in the fifties and sixties.

The idea of self-sufficient, isolated systems and a predictable and mechanistic interpretation of function was encouraged by Descartes (1596–1650). Following the Greek notion of separate substances and qualities inhering in objects, he divided human experience into primary and secondary qualities and relegated seemingly unmeasurable experience—sound, color, texture, smell, associations and the imaginative process itself—to secondary status, a not-quite-respectable nether world of subjectivity and sensation. The primary attributes of nature were those that could be consistently measured and therefore governed by universal law. Accordingly, the figure (or outline), location and mass of an object were elevated to pri-

mary status and endowed with independent self-sufficiency. The classical physics of Newton (1647–1727) posited a nature whose relevant grammar was the position and momentum of a system located in an absolute space. It was assumed that position and momentum could be accurately determined and that if the state of a system at one position could be specified then the future state of the system could also be predicted.

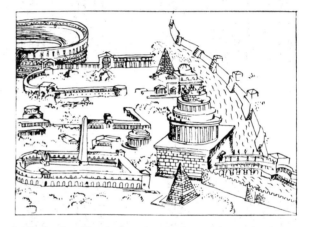

Le Corbusier. Sketch. In spite of scant evidence supporting his view, Le Corbusier propagandized the rationalist position by stating that the eye sought the simplicity of pure Euclidean solids. (*Courtesy of Fondation Le Corbusier,* © *SPADEM, Paris/VAGA, New York 1980.*)

Ludwig Hilberseimer. Project for a skyscraper city, north-south street, about 1927. Rationalist mythology in the twen-

ties led to urban images of regimented predictability. (*Courtesy of Hans Wingler.*)

Magnification of the point of a tungsten needle. A three-dimensional atomic event recorded on a camera plate at an instant too brief to imagine—an uncanny order that is currently beyond our grasp. Nature seems patient of as many systems of geometries as we can discover. At this time who can say which warrants the highest metaphysical status in ordering the world? (*Photo by Dr. Erwin W. Müller.*)

The impress of Newtonian science with its closed systems, free of impinging forces and the Cartesian denigration of sense contents can be seen in the architecture of the rationalist reformers of the International Style. The don't-touch-me perfection of their white architecture, the insistence on homogeneous systems of pure geometric forms and structures, independent of site or locale, and their reductive functionalism, all attest to Cartesian-Newtonian underpinnings. The cosmology that enabled the rationalist Moderns to proffer cubes, rectangles and other Euclidean forms as a universal visual language and to preach a determinist functionalism as the most real and most responsible ground for design also borrowed from classical aesthetics. Renaissance humanism transmitted the idea that the ideal and the beautiful resided in certain mathematic ratios and supposedly superior Euclidean figures imposed on architecture and the landscape.

But science has gradually dissolved the foundations of these views. Non-Euclidean geometries have been invented and found necessary to describe the physical world. In our own century physical science has been postulating ideas that help us accommodate the diversity of order suggested by an architecture of additions, remodeling and user participation. After formulation by Heisenberg, Bohr and others, the principles of indeterminacy and uncertainty have become cornerstones of contemporary physics.

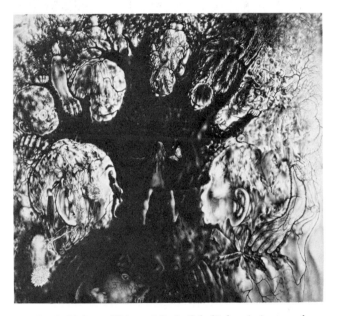

Pavel Tchelitchew. *Hide and Seek.* Tchelitchew's image of vibrating metamorphosis seems based on a radical reconstruction of space and time, and suggests a high degree of unpredictability. The tree becomes a hand, children melt into trees, the sky into blood vessels, the figure reverses with the ground and is a vibrating extension of it. The transformations in the painting are a metaphoric interpretation of what actually happens in nature as examined by recent science. (*Collection, The Museum of Modern Art, New York, Mrs. Simon Guggenheim Fund.*)

Whether or not the uncertainty principle retains its current applicability in the future, it does seem to help us now to cope with some observations about life on our planet, foremost that the earth and everything on it is changing and that the physical world apparent to human view is not entirely predictable.

The Pantheon, Rome. A pair of bell towers rested most inappropriately on the Pantheon from 1632 to 1883 when they were removed. Major features of an armature's framework, done by an architect, might also be revised, as I am suggesting in the illustration of armature with stupa changed. (*Drawing by Herb Greene. Adapted from the slide archives, College of Architecture, University of Kentucky.*)

It is not surprising that in this same century the chance combinations of the Dadaists, Cubists and Surrealists have become a vital aesthetic issue for artists. After relativity, the concepts of indeterminacy and uncertainty have become pervasive influences in aesthetics and the social sciences. Heisenberg's indeterminacy hypothesis states that either the position or the momentum of a system can be specified with precision but not both. This means that the more accurate the measurement of one term the less accurate the other. Their relationship is reciprocal. Further, position and momentum are not always the relevant grammar of a system. Energy and time, the spin of a system and other variables may become more descriptive. The classical idea that the future state of a system can be predicted has given way to the uncertainty principle, which states that given the maximum possible information about a system at any specific time, one still cannot uniquely predict the future state of the system. Modern theory leaves open a multiplicity of future states.

One outcome of the new science has been to qualify or completely alter our traditional beliefs in uniformity, objectivity and the suppos-

edly immutable laws of nature. Interest in final causes gives way to directing one's attention to particularities of situation and the recognition of what, to human perception, appears as chance or the quality shared by unexpected, random or contingent events. For example, instead of believing as did Freud that certain symbols in dreams held the same meaning for all subjects, social scientists now search for connections between behavior, meaning and language of particular individuals or cultural groups. Scientists and artists alike are prepared to create partial solutions and are increasingly ready to accept indeterminacy, uncertainty and chance because these characteristics are taken to be inescapable components of the human perception of reality. Possibly, the uncertainty principle may be misconstrued in its application to life, and in the future for all we know, give way to modifications that have often befallen scientific generalizations. At the present, however, our society has yet to effectively grasp indeterminacy and contingency, particularly in architectural aesthetics. In the preceding millenia we have imprinted ourselves with ideas about permanence and schemes of order as if we existed in a perfect and changeless world, a state of mind illustrated today in hi-tech architecture that tries to defy change, its aim being to appear "forever" as pristine and unmarked as the day it was built. The aging process is rejected and when it occurs is considered an imposition on the building.

Nevertheless the world is subject to change and to cultural juxtapositions and mismatches. In our time of instant communication isolated cultures are becoming rare. We view developing countries as different from the technologically developed nations. We witness the demoralization of societies by the sudden influx of technologies that disrupt age-old cultural patterns as one outcome of the differences. But history shows that cultural juxtapositions have always occurred and that synthesis as well as dislocation may result. From our widening understanding of natural ecologies and of human societies, we are beginning to appreciate the value of protecting the various symbol systems of different cultures. Each is a part of the social-ecological web. When we destroy these webs

Armature with stupa-like corner. Grading from solid to transparent like a rock-cut temple undergoing metamorphosis into a glassy crystal, this armature acts as an interface between a public street and private apartments which use air rights over the armature and part of the block's interior courtyard. The surfaces between lintels and beams invite infill with citizens' creations. Major alterations to this armature may be initiated by users or designers according to procedures established for on-going evaluation and change. (*Drawing by Herb Greene.*)

we limit the possibilities for new syntheses and face an ultimate sterilization of culture as well as the more immediate problem of integrating rootless populations. As a new awareness requires us to accept increasing degrees of indeterminacy, the clash of cultures becomes accepted and the mingling of diverse forms becomes a design necessity.

For at least sixty years the arts have reflected a growing interest in expressing various degrees of the unpredictable. Segments of the public have accepted its concommitant forms ranging from the drip paintings of Jackson Pollock to the ballets of Merce Cunningham in which dancers, scenic designers and composer of the musical score conceive their respective parts independently and simply present them contemporaneously on the same stage.

My personal bias toward the unpredictable does not admit its unalloyed use. It is not possible to build by unpredictability alone an organization of cues in an image that will elicit the harmony required for a response of depth and complexity. The image is a matrix of cues to which previously learned meanings can be attached. The purpose of an armature as image is to produce depth of meaning and intensity of feeling by making appropriate combinations of cues. Integrated within the pattern of a harmonized framework, uncertainty and chance show events not controlled by predetermined human systems, a reminder against hubris and complacency and a model of teleological understanding rather than a reversion to chaos. Of course, the attitude of accepting extreme degrees of chance in design may again become

The armature shown in this illustration has been altered at a later time to remove the opaque stupa-like tower at the left end in favor of a glassed-in lift to the roof garden. The transparent portico now announces a prominent entrance at an important point of pedestrian circulation. (*Drawing by Herb Greene.*)

fashionable as it did in the art Happenings of the sixties, but the intensity of an art or architectural image does not ultimately reside in attitudes. It resides in cues symbolizing already organized experiences with deeply integrated meaning that can be sympathetically combined, however surprising the combination may initially appear.

Artists and theorists have often seen scientific interpretation of indeterminacy and uncertainty as reasons for human alienation. They have chosen to interpret this to mean that human determinations are not controlled by our will, that one object of the universe is as valuable as the next, and that our ability to look at reality from within is a romantic and misleading tendency. The consequence of these beliefs is for the artist to present his subject matter in the mode of a determinist scientist, a disinterested recorder of random events who has somehow stepped outside himself to make observations: anything more subjective would betray the irresponsible freedom of romanticism. But any matter or subject, even scientific, cannot be mastered as science demands because, whatever it is, it opens perspectives of the world that are beyond complete determination. Nor can we remain free of value judgments. As organic creatures we choose between sunlight and soot. Both evolution and culture cause us to value some things over others. What we need for the armature hypothesis is not an artificial detachment but belief in the power of imagination.

If making, combining and reconstituting things, and our contemplation of the process, can acquire the status of a desired public activity, if we can relinquish worn-out views of homogeneous architectural styles, if we can enjoy the diversity of things held together in a poetic frame that helps us to integrate the unexpected, then armatures and the collage mode of their elaboration can become a celebration of what Anton Ehrenzweig calls "libidinous realism"—which loses the self in the world without needing either to renounce or master the world.

Modern utilitarians tend to see architecture as a neutral backdrop to life, not demanding any effort from humankind so that we are free to pursue "higher goals" that often tacitly assume escapist motives. To utilitarians, the need to build, repair, elaborate and renew the city by the armature strategy may seem a kind of Hermann Hesse bead game. To others, it may seem an atavistic mode lifted out of the cities of Chartres and Uxmal and grafted on the welfare arm of the modern state in order to give people something to occupy their time. We must recognize that there is a side to life that refuses to be grounded in utility and that may well be likened to a game. Although "game" means amusement, diversion and manipulation, it can also be associated with finding elegant, economic, skillful solutions and with heuristic learning by which the development of the individual is nourished. One task for civilization is to create outlets that foster creative inconvenience. When we admit to the organic pattern of renewal and decay and include the artful expression of these realities into the objectives of shaping our built environment, our throw-away society will have integrated an ancient insight and our civilization will approach a new level of maturity.

Above. Through its annual metamorphoses, the Corn Palace in Mitchell, South Dakota, sustains the image of the castle, a pleasure palace rising out of broad farmland. The metaphor of the castle, imbedded in the mythology of many cultures, emerges again in the festival building of this midwestern town. (*Photo courtesy of The Goin Company, Mitchell, S.D.*)

Below. This armature, with op art surfacing that can be replaced with other patterns over long-term cycles, is inspired by the Corn Palace. Windows of graduating size and towers of varying widths present a familiar historic base of tower-and-window as well as a more abstract composition of solid-and-void to encourage a multiplicity of responses. (*Drawing by Herb Greene.*)

Above. Detail of an urban armature. A transparent roof protects a slate-faced pylon for chalk drawings and impromptu commentary. In the background are solid walls and reliefs of citizens' art. (*Drawing by Herb Greene.*)

Below. Armature with historic windows. The ground floor is fully open to allow more opportunities for access. Color is chosen to harmonize with nineteenth century buildings nearby. The seemingly suspended stream of historic windows harmonizes with the time-stream metaphor of the landform image, as well as with the existing buildings at the right. (*Drawing by Herb Greene.*)

Above. Armature for public services. (Detail with elevator.) An armature for public services for the southwestern United States. The long-lasting core, here incorporating metaphors of regional land forms and layered with allusions to pertinent historic architecture, is gradually encrusted with citizens' crafts and arts. Important trees, fountains and pools are available to the public as is outdoor space for gatherings and exhibitions. Connected to the ceremonial core, which is used for circulation, galleries and restaurants, there are buildings designed by individual architects to house various branches of government. In contrast to the "earthy" mass of the core are large openings, which permit people to read the spaces within and to see connected departments. (*Drawings by Herb Greene.*)

Above. Regional archaeology can inspire image references of place as in this armature for an urban stage set. Here a local mill is reconstituted as a wall framework to be filled in with indeterminate additions. Glazed tile on a concrete wall recreates trees and hills, screens a day-care center and creates a backdrop for a downtown farmers' market. (*Drawing by Herb Greene.*)

Below. Armature with historic masonry. A wall of heavy "historic" masonry dissolves into glass architecture with constructivist columns and becomes a contemporary expression of free space and lightness. Among other possibilities there is the potential for reading "one era changing into another." These old-new backgrounds give different meanings to the ornamental details added by citizens and professional artists. (*Drawing by Herb Greene.*)

Above. In this armature with castle ruin, anthropomorphic curves in some of the towers show a surrealist meld of architecture and body form. These curves are buildable with current technologies in concrete, masonry and epoxy mortars and would do much to engender mystery, empathy and a dreamlike ambience. The armature is designed as a focus for a two-story private sector building of indeterminate design indicated by the line crossing the rendered form. (*Drawing by Herb Greene*.)

Below. Laycock School murals by David Cashman, Roger Fagin and the children of Laycock School, Islington, London. More than 320 students were given silk screen prints of these wall panels, on which they were asked to paint designs. Sixteen were chosen. On a high wall such as this, final installation is accomplished by professionals. It is notable here that the bricks of the building are an integral part of the design, rather than being disguised as they often are in painted murals. (*Photo courtesy of David Cashman.*)

Above and opposite page. Ethnic and territorial issues can be raised to the level of art on an armature, as in the *Wall of Respect* and the *Wall of Truth.* In an armature way of building, these murals, and parts of the buildings such as cast iron doorways and bay windows, might have become the neighborhood's historic nucleus. (*Photos by Nanine Hilliard Greene.*)

Right. Contemporary with Maybeck's collage architecture at the First Church of Christ Scientist is Fonthill, a "château" near Doylestown, Pennsylvania, built between 1908 and 1910 by Dr. Henry Chapman Mercer. Made almost entirely of reinforced concrete by unskilled workers, the structure is adorned with Mercer's own ceramic designs. The diversity of tiles, set in vaults, beams, mantles and reveals, suggests the possibility of many individual contributions to the ornament of an architectural frame on which historicist references can be read by a wide audience. Combinations like the pointed window next to an arched window show mnemonic choice rather than arbitrary inclusion. The expression of materials with integrity, and the distortion of expected proportions indicate a creative context for historic allusions which transcend the trappings of taste and class. Mercer's work reveals values that can be considered among the aims of armatures: user inquiry into historic allusion, an authentic and aesthetic use of materials and construction techniques, and a bridge between folk and fine art. (*Photo: Fonthill Museum of the Bucks County Historical Society.*)

At the Louden Nelson Community Center's mural-in-progress, Santa Cruz, California, Jeff Oberdorfer, architect, muralist and producer, transforms the blank side of a building into a *trompe d'oeil* stage set for outdoor activities. Seeking grants to finance the project, consulting with neighborhood residents on the design and enlisting local youths as painters, Oberdorfer's role resembles that of the facilitator for an armature. (*Photo by Jeff Oberdorfer.*)

Simon Rodia's towers, Watts, Los Angeles, California. I emphasize folk art because it embodies an authenticity of feeling that has been in decline in architectural ornament since the rise of industrialized building and I am using folk art as an example of the expression of direct feeling that could be recovered in ornamenting armatures. (*Photo by Nanine Hilliard Greene.*)

Folk surrealism by Henry Dorsey. Tire and dolls placed by the road next to Dorsey's house, Brownsboro, Kentucky. A nostalgic lamentation in which tire frame and contents are given equal importance and are sources of unconscious meaning and spontaneous associations. Folk artists often display works on their property for the public to see. It is my belief that folk artists like all artists, hope their work will last for posterity. For such work to be self-consciously contributed to or preserved on an armature would not mean a loss of innocence. Today, Dorsey's work is being eroded by weather, vandalism and neglect. Encased in glass or otherwise weatherproofed, this assemblage might have become a personal comment in a public armature. (*Photo by Nanine Hilliard Greene.*)

6 Architecture as a "Responsibly Limited Tool"

Excerpts from the tape of a workshop on whether an unused city school can become a neighborhood armature.

Ellen Bower: *"I live on Alder Street and from my backyard the old gym looks like a prison. What's more, it cuts the sun out of my yard."*

Celia Stokes: *"I taught here twenty-six years and never realized neighbors felt that way. Whatever we do, I want to see community services for the elderly put in here."*

John Dietz, facilitator: *"Since our architects have been consulting with developers and have been looking at structural conditions, perhaps it's time to hear their report."*

Sandra Kropotkin, chairperson: *"Joe, you have the floor."*

Joe Riley, architect: *"We can go two ways—one, turn the auditorium and arcade into a privately funded shopping area and theater. Howard Enterprises has approached us about becoming co-developers. Second, we can use first floor classrooms and lunchroom space for publicly supported health and recreation services, even food services. As for the gym, it's in such bad condition, I'd recommend tearing it down."*

Ellen B.: *"Alder Street will bloom!"*

J. M. Sterne, city controller: *"By using the main part for public services, this armature qualifies for funds under Community Rehab CB11 and R12, as we're doing with several others built around unneeded schools."*

Dietz: *"A good point, Jim. Now several students came tonight from Wagner High. Tom . . . Becky . . ."*

Tom Amato: *"If the gym is torn down, we'll need four outside basketball nets to replace the ones we've been using . . ."*

Becky Chapman: *"The Hands-On Club would like to re-cover some of the floors with mosaics like what was done at Northside Armature . . ."*

Riley: *"Fine! We'll put you on the list of craftpersons. Now, we haven't heard any ideas yet for the second floor."*

John Hoffer, neighbor: *"Three self-build apartments for live-in caretakers, is what I'd say. I'm still fair with tools and Marge wants to get out from under the old homestead."*

Riley: *"The cost of remodeling both first and second floors at the same time will probably be more than we can afford. It will be easier to get money for the first floor service area."*

Hoffer: *"But folks living in the building will cut down on vandalism."*

Sandra K.: *"Housing for seniors in the neighborhood qualifies for extended tax benefits. Maybe we can swing it."*

IN much of this book, I have discussed the desired aesthetic impact of architectural armatures. I am also concerned with their social impact and believe the two to be inextricably connected. I would like, in this chapter, to offer the architect some foundation for my belief that people in affluent countries are ready to ornament their built environment.

Since citizen additions and citizen art are by their very nature decentralized, diverse and individualistic, it is impossible to declare any one way of organizing an armature as the only or right way. Possibilities are innumerable and the field is wide open to invention. At best I present here examples of how a few architects and artists as "producers" have made embryonic beginnings for a new way to design and build, and reasons for doing so.

In his book, *Tools for Conviviality*, Ivan Illich proposes guidelines for responsibly limited tools. He speaks of tools that guarantee individuals the right to work with independence and imagination. A convivial tool allows the user to express his meaning in action. While the tool may be a highly developed piece of technology, it must be scaled to allow its use by many autonomous people. With this definition of tools, Illich conceives of a labor-intensive, yet modern, mode of production that is not a throwback to pre-industrial society. It is rather a balance between tools to solve specific demands, such as large machines for moving earth or locks to navigate rivers, and enabling tools such as skill saws, hand-held computers, and small multiuse fork lifts and tractors which foster self-realization in terms of purposes chosen by the user. According to Illich, responsibly limited tools must be rapidly developed in order to prevent impending economic breakdown and social malaise caused by decreasing resources and the failure of the dominant mode of industrial production to allow for self-realization

Although Illich's analysis is particularly directed to developing countries, what he says also applies to the developed countries. Continuing unemployment in Europe; over 35% unemployment among black teenagers in the urban U.S. in 1979; and larger numbers of older retired people or people with spare time make the question of creative jobs not only an aesthetic but economic urgency as well. I believe it is time the architectural and building profession consider how to respond to this situation. We are at a point in much urban architecture where non-user decision makers, representing large public and private organizations, produce only large scale impersonal buildings that allow no participation for the small user, builder, craftsman or artist.

Financing and marketing mass production articles takes precedent over quality. I like to equate the mass-produced tomato with mass-produced architecture. In order to reduce labor and increase profits, technicians have developed a tough-skinned tomato that can withstand the rigors of a mechanical tomato picker and automated processing. By 1976 these machines cost more than seventy-five thousand dollars. Such capital investment required tomato growers to control huge acreages and finally to own processing plants in order to cut financial risks due to weather and fluctuations in markets. Before the introduction of these machines in 1970 there were 4,000 tomato growers. In 1976 there were 597, and supermarket tomatoes, though available year around, are higher in price, pale and tasteless. I tell this tomato story because what has happened to the tomato has happened to architecture: labor-saving production has become so "efficient" it no longer produces what it started out to produce. Just as supermarket tomatoes have become pale, juiceless squares, so architecture has become stacked-up cubes that nourish neither our minds nor emotions.

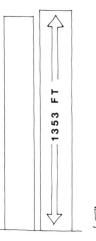

The New York World Trade Center with its gargantuan verticality has about the same energy requirements as does a city of 100,000. The half hour required for elevator transport from the upper floors during rush hours preempts lunch hour shopping and noon-time variety for workers. Similarly, the oil tanker, which each year becomes more horizontally enormous, does not take into account the social or environmental consequences of its size. I would call both irresponsibly unlimited tools.

There are other parallels between mass-produced food and mass-produced buildings and what the process has done not only to the final product but to the lives and environments of those who once farmed and built. Wendell Berry in his book, *The Unsettling of America*, combines passion with facts to show the cost of increasingly automated food production in terms of lives and resources. It takes generations of careful work, traditionally best accomplished by family farms, to foster perfect soils. In Japan and Switzerland, farms still possess a high productivity and aesthetic value, an ordered diversity of fields, animals, trees, crops, houses and tools, the result of deeply established cultures which understand the nature of the land. Industrial farming is only concerned with quantity and profits.

In order to maximize production and centralize profits, agribusiness and its supporting agencies have developed technology and undertaken practices that are damaging both to ecological systems and human lives. Soils are depleted by monoculture crops and gradually rendered useless by chemical fertilizers and pesticides. Only land that is amenable to large machines (contributing to waste, erosion, overly compacted soil) is farmed. The governing mythology is that as few people as possible should be involved in food production. Hundreds of thousands of families and individuals who farmed as a vocation because farming traditionally offered values such as independence, closeness to nature and involvement with timeless and necessary work, have been driven off the land by increasing automation and capitalization requirements. Technological exploitation has become a pattern of destruction to earth and culture.

The armature concept of design has similarities to Wendell Berry's plea for the conservation of small farms and his identification of work with culture. By restructuring the building process in accordance with principles of diversity rather than simplism, an armature way of building will reinstate craftwork in a context that contributes to culture. As responsibly limited tools, armatures are to be conceived to facilitate this end and will be reshaped and cared for over the years to give later generations the

Hilton Palacio Del Rio, San Antonio, Texas. The contractor used a mass-production system rather like the assembly line of the automobile industry. Designed to save months of construction time, enabling the hotel to be opened for Hemisfair 1968, individual rooms were constructed on the ground complete with furniture in place and lifted into position by a giant crane. What would seem to be a triumph of American know-how reduced the role of most production line workmen to near-mindless drones. Each man did one routine task, right down to the laborer who stuck mass-produced pre-glued oil paintings to the walls by use of a location template. The proliferation of non-convivial tools has destroyed value placed on individual acts of craftsmanship. The laborer is forced to sell *time* rather than acts of craft. (*Photo from Tell-Pics, San Antonio, Texas.*)

same opportunities. Like farming technology, building technology has almost eliminated the individual craftsman as well as the craft family. Modern buildings, erected with new time-and-labor-saving techniques, have reduced workers to menials and caretakers of machines.

Even if oil or other forms of energy are plentiful in the future, and they certainly may not be, it still may be a mistake to continue to build and farm in an increasingly automated fashion. If we take into account the thousands excluded from the building and farming processes, two

83

Some men and women enjoy relatively heavy construction work such as this brick paving done by a woman. An armature way of building deliberately provides for a wide range of physical work, from construction suited to strong men to light and intricate work for those with less muscle, and even opportunity for contributions from children, the handicapped and elderly, a far cry from today's buildings which generally provide work only for able-bodied men and women. (*Photo by Nanine Hilliard Greene.*)

of humankind's oldest forms of work, and if we take into account the drab and destructive side effects to our environment, we may come to see that what is technically possible is not always good for land, food, buildings or people. There is a difference between technological possibilities which ignore consequences harmful to society or individuals and technological possibilities which are concerned with beneficial consequences. We have to account for how technologies affect the physical health and psychological satisfactions of individuals and society and the health of the natural world of which we are an integral, responsible part. Translating this into architecture, armatures are an attempt to set up a building process in which technological possibilities are compatible with cultural, economic and psychological benefits for citizens.

This, I believe, is what Illich means by a "responsible tool"—a tool or building that does not accomplish only what is technologically possible but takes into account the wider benefits to society and to the individual. So far, we have not expected the building process to organize itself to give work or creative outlet to the larger citizenry, but only to an ever-smaller proportion of construction workers. Nor have we set about to invent a socio-technology in which the heaviest labor is done by machines designed to minimize pollution and in which uniquely human contributions of arts and crafts are incorporated. There have been other times when almost everyone, including women, children and the elderly, contributed to the built environment. Today our system cuts out a whole range of persons. By concentrating on high technology alone, we are turning ourselves, at best, into a nation of repairpersons—and not very good ones at that. I would not dare to estimate the value of lost imagination, unused ingenuity, wasted inventiveness. An armature intends to be a "responsible tool," inaugurating a building process open to a wide range of people whose creative abilities are now excluded by the building system.

The dramatic ethnic character of paving from Portugal and Mexico could be achieved in citizens' craft on and around an armature. Blocks fabricated on tables indoors and assembled later will avoid backbreaking work. (*Photos by Nanine Hilliard Greene.*)

Illich uses the word "limited" in referring to socially desirable tools. An armature will be limited in that it will leave the basic structure deliberately unfinished and open-ended in such a way that others can add to it. The armature process will not take advantage of all the technological possibilities available at a given time but will consciously limit design and construction in compliance with social and cultural goals. The rights of citizens to contribute their own ingenuity and talents will intentionally restrict the technological process of building.

I believe that today's increase in crafts and home hobbies are the result of citizens exercising the right to use their ingenuity. Eric Hoffer, America's longshoreman philosopher, points out in his provocative study on mass movements that people in an affluent society who do not have the opportunity for creative work or useful action are dangerously liable to be swept up in "desperate and fantastic shifts" in order to give meaning to their lives. Except in the privately owned house, it seems to me the built environment is offering fewer and fewer people opportunity for creative work or useful action. Society can no longer be blind to the political implications of the way we build: to exclude as many citizens as possible, to cut them off from creative outlets in keeping with their abilities is to take away the opportunity for a particularly lasting form of useful action in the public realm. This continued deprivation can, as Hoffer says, lead to desperate action as people seek to find meaning for their lives. I don't say the crafts and arts are the only answer to meaningless lives, yet it seems that the creative process as exercised by individuals has vital implications for the state of mind of a whole society. In a country where prosperity has been the rule rather than the exception we can afford to try new ways to make possible creative work in the public realm.

The weakening and sometimes disappearance of older social structures such as the large extended family, the ethnic enclaves, or the churches, has frequently left the individual without an organization to identify with and defenseless against mass pressures. To offer citizens a choice between the too-large or authoritarian social structure which obviates any power or involvement on the part of the individual or the too-individualistic private environment is to miss a way of designing and building that intentionally creates medium-sized social structures that might, to some extent, substitute for the disappearing family or ethnic enclave. I am suggesting that architecture, in order to be a "responsibly limited tool," could build at a scale and with a technology that requires the formation of medium-sized social structures.

I have tried to conjecture what size organizations will be most appropriate to achieve diversity in the additions to an armature, or whether the base form of the building can be conceived first, and in going about its continuing amplification, organizations of the right size and character will evolve. In an armature, I think both may occur simultaneously. An armature cannot be accomplished by a large hierarchical corporation, nor by isolated individuals. Like the technology itself, groups for continuing the work will be "responsibly limited" in size and

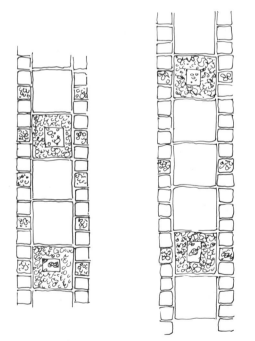

Sketch for a concrete sidewalk with individualized hand-done squares of pebble patterns. Gradually filling in the design, plain slabs can be replaced, one at a time, by handwork without rebuilding the walk. In Mexico today sidewalks such as this represent increasing mass production. I am suggesting we turn the production system around so the plain blocks represent places for creative craft work.

Brass newspapers and vegetable crates imbedded in Boston's Haymarket paving illustrate that even trash can be transformed by art and craftsmanship. (*Photo by Nanine Hilliard Greene.*)

power. Since one goal is an aesthetic of diversity, input from many small organizations rather than from a few large ones will be necessary. I see these as having social as well as aesthetic ends. Decisions will have to be made by groups of appropriate size to allow individuals to carry weight within the organization. We are already familiar with examples of built space that shape equivalent social structures: apartments produce tenant groups; blocks spawn block clubs; and a court, cul-de-sac or other well-defined area frequently encourages a small group of well-organized activists. This means that in terms of design, the architect will not only create a basic structure, but will design within it unfinished parts of the building or the open space or the neighborhood that will require limited decision-making processes. On a building, for example, the architect may design discrete bays or areas that are temporarily empty or unornamented, yet safe and attractive while waiting for a group to fill them in. On a town hall, recreation or civic building, experts or hobbyists in a particular craft—ceramics, woodworking, bricklaying, etc.—may organize themselves to fill designated space. Clubs,

schools or even classes of children can become responsible for a limited section of space, wall, or paving—if the original design intentionally encourages decision-making by small groups. On a commercial armature, small businessmen can decide on additions; in a residential area neighbors may join together to decide on the development and use of the long lived architectural elements, and of common garden space, energy sources or ornamental features. The need for numerous smaller architectural decisions will bring about not only the complex aesthetics we have been seeking, but will make necessary small, automonous groups of citizens. These mediating groups can play a vital role in giving identity to the individual and can act as advocates in matters between the individual and a city or other large entity.

In *The Oregon Experiment*, Christopher Alexander and other architects propose a planning process in which small groups of users are made responsible for initiating, financing and evaluating performance of limited areas of new construction. I am in agreement when he says, "as projects get larger, user representation becomes clumsy and the building itself tends to be impersonal. . . . When it comes to the gigantic project, they cannot see themselves personally related to it, so they discuss it very abstractly, and make quick decisions. In short, even at the highest levels of decision making, people feel remote from the design of huge ventures. It is the small projects which capture their imagination, and emotion, and involvement."

In an armature, a pluralist society can be expressed visually. The execution and appreciation of complexity and diversity in architecture and art makes more real our ideal of political pluralism, and can make a reality of small decision-making and working groups. The U.S. is a country based on a body of political theory which, with all our shortcomings, we have come close to approaching in reality. These traditions support the formulation of a theoretical basis for armatures. I see the armature way of building as being compatible with our political aspirations. Not to try to carry out these ideals in the built environment as well as in our political life seems to me an abrogation of our responsibilities as architects, builders and citizens.

Armatures also require a distinction between the meanings of unsatisfying labor and satisfying work. In the 1880's, the attitude that work was undertaken to fulfill personal needs of self-expression and self-justification took ideological form in the arts and crafts movement in England. In protest by social critics and artists against the ugliness and injustices of industrial civilization, the movement spread to Europe and the United States and lasted until the 1914–1918 World War. Its adherents, particularly concerned with housing and the artifacts of domestic life, claimed that industrialization produced poor quality and tasteless products as well as frustration and alienation among workers. Traditional cottages in England and Germany, California bungalows, Mission furniture, pottery and wallpapers showing the impress of handwork are typical of the arts and crafts legacy. However, by the mid-1920's, industrial corporations were seeking international markets for their products. Scientific management with its emphasis on standardization of work methods, tools and parts, its division of labor into repetitive specialized tasks, and its time and motion studies transformed the role of the worker as well as the product. The continuance of ethnic identity and origins of form associated with traditional crafts gave way to the economics of centralization and the profits of mass production. The theory was that instead of spending long demeaning hours to produce the handmade, a worker was to spend short hours tending machine production. The result to the worker: more leisure and money to enjoy the collective bounty of increased goods, a situation that has come true to considerable extent. Except that beyond enjoyment we now find ourselves and our environment overwhelmed, even degraded, by the flood.

It is fascinating to see the shift in attitudes among design professionals of the 1920's. Walter Gropius, director of the Bauhaus, a school of design established originally to enhance provincial craft production in the Saxe-Weimar area of Germany, had preached the craft ethic. He declared, as late as 1922, that wood was the material best suited to the expression of national aspirations. Under the Expressionist ethos which lasted from 1919 to 1923 Gropius and Hans Meyer produced timber designs and built a log house with a dark, carved wood interior. In touch with the local population's dependence on cottage industries and handcrafts, the Bauhaus emphasized true crafts, individual work in carpentry, wood carving and pottery. By 1924, responding to German businessmen and an increasingly rationalist temper, Gropius swept out traditional attitudes toward crafts with the "new objectivity" and the Bauhaus began its international influence over the design professions. In the building process even ornament was taken out of people's hands because of the need to standardize and to use factory-made products.

In the twenties architects even romanticized mass production. On one of Le Corbusier's early studios, handcrafted frames were actually painted to look as if they were mass-produced steel! However, machine efficiency, new technologies, and consumerism soon became sirens to the Western industrial nations leading, as we have seen, to the enigmas of industrial pollution and the depletion of resources. The hope was that technology would provide us with new and wonderful materials with which we could produce new and better buildings. Yet, as our building technology has expanded, inflation and an economic system which encourages quick profits have contributed, ironically, to boring standardization, the cheap and the expedient, and a general decline in the quality of our cities.

It wasn't until the mid-1960's that a new craft movement appeared in the United States, a manifestation of a counter-culture outside the mainstream. The return to crafts and in some cases to farming by the college graduate sons and daughters of successful businessmen was a reaction against the avalanche of products for consumption and the abuse of land. It was an attempt to return to careful work for the creation of things that last.

Laboring to surround ourselves with ugly objects, unaesthetic buildings, air, noise and trash pollution, and laboring in occupations that suppress our creativity have all contributed to a lowering of the quality of life. This, coinciding with economic affluence, symbolizes a trend toward the absurd in technical societies.

Hannah Arendt in *The Human Condition*, describes differences between "labor" and "work." Labor is effort expended on material as preparation for its eventual consumption. Work, she holds, is the process of making that occurs when a new thing with enough durability to remain in the world as an independent entity has been added to the human artifice. According to Arendt, to be alone with the "idea," the mental image of the thing to be; to gain mastery over material and a relationship to tools where tools remain servants, unable to replace the guiding hand, unlike machines which demand that the laborer serve them, are the prerequisites of work. As a way of redirecting at least some portion of the mainstream building process more in keeping with our socio-political ideals and traditions, an armature seeks to offer people a place and a way to work, not labor, on the public artifice.

An enormous urge for the unique object and for creative work has been covered over by industrialization. But boredom with the job, shorter hours, more education and better health have given people time and desire to turn to craftsmanship. Unfortunately evidence of this is rarely seen in the public environment but is hidden away in private homes and back yards or brought out for Sunday craft fairs. I see an armature way of designing and building as architecture's reaction to unsatisfying consumption. The sheltering of craft work in a public landmark can be a bulwark of permanence not only for the object but for the individual and the community. To give some idea of the time and energy that architects might be using to advantage, it is estimated that one out of every four persons in the United States is seriously involved in some form of arts or crafts. In a population of over 200 million, this means that something like 50 million people are looking to the creative arts for satisfaction. Estimates are that around 375,000 of them are professionals—people who earn their living in the arts and crafts. Many young people in high schools want to become artists, craftspersons, musicians, dancers, etc. Recently a TV commentator deplored their "unrealistic" attitude and urged

that the schools reorient them toward a "practical" way of making a living. It was pointed out they are living in a dream world and that they had better become trained for computer programming, machine tending and appliance repair skills. The program unwittingly revealed a well of creative talent soon to be discarded by society because there will be few jobs waiting.

To motivate citizens to work on, or in any way contribute to, an armature, the basic structure, I believe, will have to be supported by public funds and clearly be a public building. By public I mean seen as belonging to the citizens of a city, town, village, subdivision, or neighborhood. Although private corporations may pay people to have their buildings adorned, I doubt that people will contribute voluntarily to a private enterprise, or that a government entity can often use taxes to embellish a private building (although numerous public-private funding arrangments are used in rebuilding our center cities). The psychological

A professional engineer, Norman Hosie, adds detail to Yule Nissen. More retired people and people with time on their hands go in for wood carving for the sheer fun of it. (*Photo courtesy The Lexington Herald Leader.*)

needs satisfied by participation and self-realization will mean involvement in a work of generally accepted public good that allows both personal identification and self-transcendence.

Nearly all people crave to identify with some form of culture or ideal of civilization that passes beyond individual lives. That is to say our actions in the present are fortified by the belief that our efforts will not be wasted and will extend into a future capable of saving some part of our contribution. Forms of this identity, whether vague or explicit, call for participation with a state of nationhood, home, family, tribe, religion; or with a spiritualized sense of an institution or field of endeavor such as architecture, medicine, law, etc. Expressions of this sense of transcendence often involves ritual, intention, and pattern close to the ritual, intention, and pattern that art imposes on experience. While most people are not concerned with "art" and only a few are consciously concerned with "culture," almost all are willing to participate in cultural expressions that offer the possibility of self-transcendence. We can argue that for civilization to exist at all, a sufficiency of outlets for self-transcendence must be present.

Developing an armature as a focus of place offers an appropriate example. The tendency for most of us to be loyal to the place we live is common everywhere. Although financial incentives in our society tend to make people move from one house or city to another, loyalty to neighborhood, town, county remains strong. Often those who contribute to the building and care of the hometown identify with it to such an extent they refuse to accept better-paid jobs elsewhere. Nevertheless, as we become an increasingly mobile population and as more people live in rented quarters, I can see an armature building as a kind of civic "home," a place in the community where, through self-realization and feelings of transcendence, one can again put down emotional roots.

Public support of the arts and crafts will not be new. In the U.S., programs during the Great Depression were substantial. The early New Deal caught a mood that permitted public subsidization of artists. Some advocates saw the program as relief similar to other emergency and temporary programs to assist an economically stricken nation. Others saw it as a permanent link between government and community life and the recognition of the importance of art in society. A few saw it as an aesthetic dead end: good art to them could only be the product of a small élite and could never be fostered in mass programs. While some readers may see analogies between implementing a citizens' arts program and the Federal Art Project (FAP) of the 1930's, important differences are intended.

The politically sensitive instrument of the FAP under the larger Works Progress Administration (WPA) could never successfully separate its role of censor and bureaucratic supervisor of public funds from the support of free thinking artists whose work patterns did not lend themselves to clocked routine. In spite of many remarkable accomplishments, the clumsiness of centralized authority and a lack of agreement on goals, methods and results disqualify the New Deal experiment as a proven forerunner for armatures. However, some aspects of the program might be studied as a model of how to set up extensive art and craft workshops. By 1940 it was estimated that over 2,000,000 adults, teens, and children attended day and night classes in 160 locations. Curriculums included 23 subjects from photography to ceramics. In one unit, 64 trained "reliefers" taught arts and crafts out of workshops traveling in trucks. Lessons learned from those Depression days could be applied to a community wishing to set up workshops for large numbers of citizens.

Unfortunately each piece of art in the FAP program had to stand on its own merits as a mural, a sculpture, an easel painting, etc. It was not intended to become part of an encompassing architectural collage, as I am suggesting, bonded by a broader context. For an armature, not all or even some of its ornament need qualify as "high art." Pieces in an assemblage, given order by artist-facilitators and supported aesthetically by a larger designed framework, overlaid with harmonies of scale and color, can have artistic value through sheer accumulation. The ever-changing record of individual commentary has interest in its own right.

The Federal Art Program essentially took its criteria from museums and galleries which single out solo work and evaluate it on its ability to stand alone against a neutral background. The specatator of this art-of-the-solo-performance is not involved in its creation, in fact, is so passive he is even told how to view it. Beginning with nineteenth century Bohemian art culture in Europe, art critics and dealers began to supply explanations of art. The same situation still exists: the solo artist, art critic and patron are caught in an art-of-reduction and abstraction (or whatever the style) explainable by theory, and the citizen viewer is instructed how to view gallery art. Status and market value of much of this art depends on the star system and an art-for-art's-sake attitude. Even outdoor art, those isolated cubes and metal sculptures we see set against the backdrop of a 60-story office building, suffers from being chosen by gallery standards. The last thing in the minds of this circle of artists and donors would be an art-of-the-unexpected which responds to particular sites, social groups, legends and events that do not depend on the exclusivity of the star system.

I do not minimize the vital role of museums and galleries in a society of people-artists. But along with seeing original and valued works and vicariously participating in culture, I believe there is a craving to become actively involved in making the unique and handcrafted product. People are saying to themselves, "How did the artist do that!" This is one reason painters go to painters' shows, photographers to photographers' exhibits, consciously aware of the artistry and knowledge and the desire to do it themselves. However, for the past century or more, Western culture has promoted the idea that only the virtuoso could create in the arts.

The concept of the artist working alone has probably reached an unhealthy imbalance in our society. There is a growing reaction which begins to place value on working with others and integrating skills and differences. Speaking of the design for the fountain at the San Francisco Hyatt House, artist-facilitator Ruth Asawa says, "I thought it was a great opportunity to show how group skills could be used to make something that people usually think of as high art— one product from one person's mind and hands. We have this egocentric idea that the artist has to do his own thing alone. Because of this I think art has become weaker in many ways and less able to satisfy us. There have always been great individuals in art, but great art has also been produced by skilled people working together. It is the idea of bringing skills together that interests me. We see this in science, in the space program, but we have lost it in art. The idea that the artist makes a drawing of what's in his head and then gives it to a fabricator who makes it isn't the same thing. There should be more interaction than that. People working together learn to do each other's thing; they have a greater understanding of the product."

Asawa's work, a reaction against the myth that only a few are talented, suggests that many works done by citizen artists could survive and prosper in a strong setting as I am suggesting in an armature building or framework. While the scale of her assemblages is small, Asawa's method is potentially useful for a program of architectural dimensions. Small private visions take on new import when incorporated in a public work. By bringing the crafts and arts out of the private realm and once again into public view we confirm the reality of our common experience of being human.

It is my hope that an armature architecture will give professional artists as well as amateurs a chance to free themselves from gallery taste by providing access to a diverse historic and aesthetic background and the challenge of changing contextual design situations. I believe that as people with diverse ethnic backgrounds work together all will become more able to read symbols from other cultures and other times. While regional uniqueness and authenticity will be grounding tenets for the metaphors of an armature, communication today, especially television, has made us less parochial and more ready to accept and understand each other's symbols without being threatened. In conceiving his surreal castles, surely the Postman Cheval must have seen photographs of Indo-Chinese and Hindu temples. Former sailor Charles Caskin makes figure sculpture that evokes memories of Assyrian reliefs and Bible

90

readings. Even a century ago the references in Victorian eclectic ornament had few bounds and German Expressionism of 1920 included architecture from India. While we reconstitute local traditions, we must at the same time take care not to fix limits in a world of cross-communication.

Asawa's fountain indicates how various correspondences with world art can be suspended successfully in an image. Literal indications of San Francisco landmarks are rendered with children's naiveté, cubist simultaneity (presenting top views next to side views) and spatial depth by varying the size of familiar objects such as cars and people. Even the drum shape of the fountain (determined by the architects for the hotel) becomes round edged and textured suggesting affinities with Asian art.

Ruth Asawa exemplifies, too, the role of the artist-facilitator. She is not only a creative artist herself, but evolves ways for others to be creative. In the U.S., the importance of this dual role is beginning to be recognized in programs

Charles Caskin, *World of Lost Art*, Yuma, Arizona. From concrete and soft stone, the artist carves images he remembers from his travels with the Navy. (*Photo by Jan Wampler.*)

Artist Ruth Asawa's fountain in front of the Hyatt on Union Square, San Francisco, has become a tourist attraction. Asawa used her own house as a workshop for people ranging in age from three to eighty-seven. For other projects she has drawn on school art classes already funded and staffed and which have a work place. The wealth of amateur art that usually disappears into private houses Asawa assembles into murals, plaques and bronze surfaces adding her own creative sense in such a way that the end product is a new community work of art in its own right. (*Photo by Skelton Photography. Courtesy Hyatt on Union Square, San Francisco.*)

undertaken jointly by federal and state agencies. For example, as in other states, the Kentucky Arts Commission and the National Endowment for the Arts make it possible for schools to employ artists and architects-in-residence. Bringing talents in such fields as painting, pottery, sculpture, design, construction, etc., projects range from murals to greenhouses. An armature will provide a place for some of this work to be seen by the public, giving students, not to mention the architects and artists, a greater sense that their work matters to a wide audience.

Art schools graduate thousands each year who have little opportunity of earning a living in art except by teaching, and recently there has been a large oversupply of candidates for available positions. The cost of maintaining university art schools has increased and more taxes are needed to subsidize students, taxes not likely to be borne unstintingly if the public sees fewer jobs available in the arts. I am suggesting that the production of individualized architecture and ornament in the public realm would create many new part-time and full-time jobs and training programs for artist-facilitators. Recently the City of Cambridge in Greater Boston passed an ordinance calling for one percent of all funds spent on any construction project (paid in full or in part by the city) to be used for

91

Detail from Ruth Asawa's fountain, Hyatt House Plaza, San Francisco. Under the direction of artist Ruth Asawa, baker's clay figures were cast in bronze. Techniques in which fragile materials, easily workable by large numbers of people, can be transformed into permanent works of art open up new possibilities for architectural ornament. (*Photo by Laurence Cuneo.*)

developing, creating and administrating public arts. This program may be a harbinger of city government's support of the arts to increase jobs, raise the quality of urban life and bring in tourist revenues.

We're eager in this country to assemble millions in public and private money to build with large capital, large machinery, manufactured materials and organized labor. Unfortunately we often can't seem to find much smaller sums for the salaries of facilitator-designers at the local level who can organize the great well of talent that resides in ordinary persons. Money for small on-going projects, money for modest salaries and materials available at the neighborhood level has been sadly hard to find. It may be, however, that an increasing surplus of young unemployed men and women, especially in the cities, and of older retired people, will be such a burden on our welfare system that in the future funds for alternatives will become mandatory. If we train people as artist-facilitators whose abilities touch off creativity in thousands of others, they will be as valuable to society, in economic terms, as those who increase the output of a factory. Rather than train people to become stylists working for manufacturers whose products are passed through the sieve of mass market taste, I believe many artists would prefer to contribute to the public artifice if such were possible. University and community arts programs are recognizing the value of arts for their contribution to new life-styles as well as the intellectual and applied uses of the arts that we have previously expected. We need now to expand the meaning of future lifestyles to include creative work on the buildings, streets, walls, schools, neighborhoods that surround us. The architect-artist as facilitator for groups of citizens produces a service to society that can gain in status and economic importance. A society determines what services and commodities are important to meet its needs. (Mental health therapy, for example, unknown fifty years ago, has become a growth profession in American society.) If our society demands work that reveals human emotion, thought and action, and if our society puts high value on the handcrafted product, then architecture, I believe, can be ready to serve these needs.

One vigorous example of citizen art is the serpentine bench around President Ulysses S. Grant's Tomb in New York. With support from the National Park Service and other organizations, artist-facilitator Pedro Silva built the armature, a sturdy winding concrete bench. Working in the summer of 1973 he organized scores of people, many from nearby Hispanic neighborhoods, who applied tile mosaics to create a work of diversity, color and excitement. Like a scroll unrolling its document of lovers, mermaids, flowers, buildings, taxis, . . . the multicolored fantasy full of good humor encircles the dour tomb. Children climb on it, tourists photograph it, lovers sit on it. Unfortunately, the program was not on-going nor attached to an on-going institution. However, five years later, while the lower portion of Grant's Tomb is spray-painted with oaths and epithets, the surrounding bench shows no vandalism—proof, at least for now, that what people identify with by building themselves, they care for and protect.

Another example is "Patchwork Plaza" in the southwest corner of Washington Square, New York. A City Arts workshop was set up by Susan Shapiro with grants from public and private sources. Children and teenagers stopped by to mold a cement paving block and decorate it with colored tile chips. With the help of a professional engineer, these triangular blocks were assembled into a lively circular area. Each block is identical in size but no two are the same and designs range from lively abstracts to peace signs, zodiac symbols, and flowers. Personal expressions of beauty, humor, anger are embedded in this small corner of New York's paved earth. By attempting to cover only a limited area of the Square in a limited time, facili-

tators and over 700 citizen-artists gained a sense of accomplishment.

As examples of citizens' art show, the work is appearing as an afterthought in an architectural setting, unrelated to its background, as isolated as a piece of gallery art. I am advocating that given form and random form come together to make a new integrated form. We are ready psychologically for architectural ornament evolving out of a democratic process. Citizens, I believe are ready to contribute their talents and yet the given and the random have not been brought together as an aesthetic whole. The architectural frame has not been provided for this to happen.

On the other hand, as we strengthen the setting for aesthetic reasons, as I am urging in an armature way of building, there is the danger of over-control and thus losing the diversity of citizen work that comes from decentralized decision making. The sense of commitment, the ethnic power and spontaneity illustrated, for example, at the *Wall of Respect* in Chicago, needs to be provided for and allowed to occur without interference on an armature. The dan-

Mosaic bench surrounding Grant's Tomb, New York. The form of the bench lacks the power, subtlety and practicality that raises Gaudi's seating at Parc Güell to a high level of art. Nevertheless these American mosaics express spontaneity and life. Perhaps in years to come they can be extended across the paving and up the base of the tomb to obliterate vandalizing graffiti—and literally engulf the building. (*Photo by Nanine Hilliard Greene.*)

Hemisfair, San Antonio, Texas, 1968. Janine Wagner, artist, collected irregular plywood scraps out of which children in the fair's nursery made individual designs, painting and pasting pieces to rectangular boards. Arranged together by the artist, these red and gold "bas-reliefs" form a visually effective tapestry large enough to be in scale with the fair's buildings. The surprise and charm of children's art reads through the order of repetitive patterns. The artist has coordinated individual pieces to make a wall design more successful than its parts. (*Photo by Nanine Hilliard Greene.*)

A youth group from Cleveland, Ohio, helps Cordia High School students in Kentucky refurbish the school floor. Limited to an assortment of surplus tiles, they have laid a mosaic pattern more interesting than the usual commercial repetitions. I include this picture, not because it shows creativity of a caliber aspired to by an armature program, but because it indicates the energy of self-help groups all over the country whose efforts can be raised to a high level of art with assistance from skilled facilitators and craftspersons. (*Photo by Frannie Millward.*)

94

Architects and artists will find innovative projects in which wood, concrete, brick, and even linoleum offer endless possibilities for groups of citizens to work together under the guidance of professionals. These examples can have far greater aesthetic impact if incorporated into buildings intentionally designed to receive them.

Floor tiles from "Caerulea," an imaginary civilization created by artists Eleanore Bender and Eleanor Rappe, Sausalito, California. Fascination with archaeology and the embellishment of history is seen in designs from "Caerulea—Ruins and Restorations," an exhibit of artifacts from a hypothetical lost civilization. Printmakers Bender and Rappe reveal the curious power of a mythological past on the imagination and suggest themes and techniques that can be developed for the ornamental surfaces of armatures. (*Photo by Eleanor Rappe.*)

Inman Square Fire Station, Cambridge, Massachusetts. Incised concrete blocks depicting old fire engines are fitted above the present station's doors. Under supervision by artists, both cutting and casting in concrete are methods that can be handled by citizens. (*Photo by Nanine Hilliard Greene.*)

ger of control by a strong institution is very real: already there are threats from within the National Park Service to remove the bench at Grant's Tomb as not appropriate to the solemnity of the tomb, and in Montreal during the 1976 Olympic Games the mayor bulldozed away overnight the temporary reconstruction of an historic street. Constructed for $385,000 and billed as "the world's biggest outdoor art gallery," "Corridart" was the core of an Olympics program of visual and performing arts from photography to opera. But because it demonstrated the cultural loss of graceful and historic houses that had been torn down to make room for commercial high-rises and parking, it was taken by the Mayor as intolerable political criticism.

If the basic armature structures require the investment of large sums, and some will, then federal, state and city governments will likely become involved. Enriching the public environment will warrant support from public sources, but these bodies will have to relinquish control of the use and expressive modes so that small mediating organizations can be autonomous in their decision-making. Just as neighborhood energies were focused by *The Wall of Respect,* so small beginnings have resulted in widened citizen control of other communities: in Edinburgh, Scotland, what began as one woman's efforts to arrange music lessons for underprivileged children in a low-income neighborhood has turned into the annual Craigmillar Festival and has eventually brought about neighborhood direction of large-scale physical planning and considerable improvement to the economic and cultural life of the community. In an armature way of building, there is no telling what directions a local group may take once they have organized themselves, even for such a small purpose as making a mural or section of paving.

Most important and most difficult to realize is this degree of local control. People living in a neighborhood or using an urban place should feel the long-lived features are theirs, to make, to use and pass on to posterity, and at the same time their work needs enough framework to produce a certain degree of aesthetic strength and size. It is too simple to say that the patron-

The Wall of Respect and the *Wall of Truth,* 43rd and Langley Streets, Chicago, were conceived and designed by artists William Walker, Sylvia Abernathy and others. These murals sparked consciousness, respect of self, dignity, and pride in the black community. With themes of black heroes, selected by the community, Walker began an art form that was accessible to the poor and privileged alike. Divided into sections, the Walls were created by some 18 artists and community activists between 1967 and 1969. Within a few years the buildings were razed and remnants of the murals moved to Malcolm X College, but permanence had not been envisioned for the Walls. Their real purpose was to promote dialogue, even if only temporary, within the community. An outgrowth of energies mobilized for the Walls is the Martin Luther King, Jr. Community Service Center, where artist Eugene Eda plans a porcelain enamel mural dedicated to the first *Wall of Respect. (Photo by Nanine Hilliard Greene.)*

Corridart, an art fair on Sherbrooke Street, Montreal, 1976. Workmen rip down Corridart's newly constructed plywood replicas of old houses which were demolished to make room for commercial highrises and parking lots. The historic reconstruction was ordered razed by the Mayor as an unacceptable criticism of the city's renewal program. Elements of an armature must have strong support from sources other than government and business groups alone, which have gotten us where we are today—in a position of destroying the irreplaceable historic, aesthetic, regional and social fabric of the city. *(Photo by George Cree.)*

95

Three incarnations of the Corn Palace, Mitchell, South Dakota. Covered with kernels from a variety of corn—yellow, red, and brown—this festival building is decorated each year by an artist in celebration of the annual harvest. Local farmers grow special corn, and great pictorial panels are made of kernels to cover the building's walls and towers. In some years a wholesome fantasy and in others an expression of corniness (in its obvious allusions as well as in its kernels), the Corn Palace expresses mid-American qualities of ambition and naïveté. I am particularly fascinated by the 1904 and 1905 editions which, in the tinted photographs, recall the childlike-and-sophisticated images of architecture by the painters Klee and Hundertwasser. Not truly a harbinger of people's art, since the designs are made by a single artist and carried out under his direction, it nonetheless offers suggestions for an armature that could accept people's art and respond to cyclic alterations. In the past, the design didn't last long: pigeons and squirrels ate the kernels, but with today's pest repellants the fanciful Corn Palace has become a year-long sight for townspeople and tourists alike. (*Photo courtesy of the Goin Company, Mitchell, S.D.*)

age of government and business is always inimical to these aims, but the majority of people must be sure armatures are their domain and not coercive institutions in disguise.

Like Asawa's fountain, some work will be done in workshops, or at home, or in schools and institutions, and finally assembled on an armature under the guiding skills of professional artists. However, much building, art and craft can be done on the site. There will be many occasions to dramatize construction. With flood lights at night, music and food, building can become a party. Passersby, instead of peeking through knot-holes in a fence, can be provided with seats and a good view of citizens working—a moveable *son-et-lumière* of what's happening in the present and a "preview" of what's about to be. Or perhaps the architect will design certain areas as "work thea-

ters," and with the artist, evolve schedules in tune with the skills, available time and attention spans of citizen workers and audiences. Easily managed materials can be sought. Many spaces on and within the basic building can be designed as "hangers" to which theater-like additions can be conveniently added.

An armature will express action. It will no longer be only a finished image that the architect is trying to achieve. Rather, the everyday putting up and taking down, the sounds of hand tools and voices, workers with ladders and fork-lifts, or children on walkways that enable walls to be reached easily and the craft and art workshops incorporated within the buildings will together become an architecture of action. If a structure is designed from its inception to allow this to happen without inconvenience or danger to users and passersby, the action generated becomes an on-going drama.

I also see the armature designed as backdrop for concerts, plays, dances, and festivals of all kinds. It is a rare building in the U.S. that changes its façade to suit events or to be in tune with the dramatically changing seasons. One exception is the Corn Palace in Mitchell, South Dakota, which changes not only each summer but over the decades has metamorphosed several times in a way we never see in our concrete and glass cities. While the creation of tourist attractions such as this is a secondary goal of armatures, tourism, after agriculture and manufacturing, provides the most revenue in our economy. Cities with history kept intact with interesting architecture are among the most stable tourist attractions. Witness the appeal of old cities in Europe whose cores have remained relatively free of industrial incursion, and the attraction of historic cities in the U.S. such as New Orleans, Savannah and Charleston which have preserved large historic districts. A long-lived armature will gradually become an enriched historical form, quite possibly the most arresting architectural expressions of a town. As we have said, the architecture we envision suggests a broad involvement in the arts. Celebrations of theater, music, and dance, and other cultural events generated by the activity of building the armatures can draw tourists and have a positive economic impact on a city.

Pieces of art made for armatures and recycled after appropriate duration to make room for new works can become valuable marketable commodities.

New Tools

There is considerable information today on small-scale tools and building techniques for developing countries. Many tools have been invented for societies in dire need of basic shelter, food, clean water, etc. Some may be useful for building additions and ornamenting an armature. But since much of the work in a relatively affluent developed country will not be to fulfill dire need, a tool's first purpose will be to allow creativity for the worker who is enjoying the work. Ease of use by amateurs, quietness, cleanness will be some of the requirements not today demanded of construction tools that all too often contribute to air and noise pollution. As needs arise I would expect our ingenuity to continue to invent small low-energy machines that do the worst of the dirty work, leaving the worker free for more creative tasks. Many old tools are being reevaluated: the familiar wheelbarrow has been rebalanced to carry larger loads with less human effort. Renting small and large machines such as fork-lifts, dump trucks, saws, sanders and reusable forms for poured concrete have already become a good business. The fact that citizens will add their time and tal-

Armature with Op Art inspired by the Corn Palace. Clay tile facings are designed to visually warp the towers with perceptual ambiguity. The towers make niches of different proportions which encourage a variety of uses. Their lower surfaces are covered with citizens' art which is periodically renewed. An interior courtyard allows additive enclosures. (*Drawing by Herb Greene.*)

ents to the building process need not reduce the number of jobs in conventional construction. Skilled union labor will be needed for those features that call for heavy machinery or high technology. By elaborating and diversifying features normally left plain and by creating new features, new jobs will be created. Supplying materials and small tools for citizen-workers may also open up unforeseeable business opportunities. For instance, semi-handmade bricks of various design, aesthetically more pleasing than mass-produced bricks, might be made to achieve permanence, individual expressiveness, and relative flexibility. In England the price of handcrafted bricks made at local kilns is now little more than the cost of mass-produced bricks made at a centralized installation when costs of transportation are taken into account. In the 1920's, the rich variety of Frank Lloyd Wright's systems of making textured concrete block provides an example that was never fully exploited. Similar systems, appropriate to the armature strategy of combining craft with technology, could be developed in workshops or on-the-job sites.

Most important, new jobs for facilitators and "producers" will be created. It has repeatedly been shown in domestic and overseas self-help programs that the quality of work done by amateurs is directly in correlation with the quality of guidance. With talented supervision, amateurs can build with very nearly the same excellence and work at nearly the same speed as professional construction workers. As architecture develops into a "responsibly limited tool," I foresee that the architect-artist will find new opportunity to correct in some measure what Illich calls the social malaise caused by the failure of present-day building methods. The numerous examples of citizens' work we are beginning to see illustrate that the creative talent of humanity has been put aside by the mass-production process only temporarily. Through an armature way of building, architecture can offer work that brings about self-realization for a wide range of people, and buildings can be designed to receive the on-going creation of things that last.

Part Three / INTEGRATION OF ARCHITECTURE, CRAFT AND ART

7 Architectural Ornament in a New Context

This evening I visit a community workshop, a space made over from an auto salesroom. A paper-mache mock-up of a fountain and wading pool sits in the middle of the floor. On the walls are huge drawings that prove to be layouts for pavement designs. I've read about this project so I know the park surrounding the new capital armature is being ornamented by citizen craft groups throughout the state. Today forty or more people are participating in a two-way TV discussion with architects, master craftspersons, artists and others about the design. As the screen darkens a cheer goes up. Mixed with fun and enthusiasm there is a sense of seriousness. Workspace is well laid out. North skylights over big tables shed ample light on a group at work with sanders, snips and solder. I'm drawn to shelves where cast glass blocks are finished and lined up waiting to be installed on the armature. Suspended in each is a vintage engraving or bits of historical memorabilia. The oddments seem strange yet pleasurable as they float, sealed and reflecting, in and out of focus, in the watery glass.

IN the past, architectural ornament has often been thought of as the "uneconomic" parts of architecture executed for expression of their beauty alone. In classical architecture these were the fleshing out of the shaft with entasis and the molded cap and base of a Doric order. Sir John Summerson holds that these parts became obligatory by convention, like words in a sentence. Their appropriate grammatical expression gave cohesion and order. But, he says, not all ornament satisfied syntactical criteria. Gothic capitals, unlike the Doric, were often carved with foliage that did not crystalize into language. Summerson predicts that approaches to ornament in our time are likely to take two directions: one, a search for meaning in terms of iconographic and metaphoric content, or as a medium of emotional communication.

Since our world admits dissonance, complexity and unpredictability to degrees unknown in previous times, we will need, on armatures, forms of ornament to convey iconic and metaphoric meanings commonly understood by people with diverse backgrounds. At the same time, while we will not reproduce the linear and repeatable grammar of a Doric order, we will still need formal receptacles that mediate our responses and hold together the diversity of citizens' work. We will also need an ornament of emotional communication that speaks of a situation in which the cultural, social and political consciousness of the producers is not

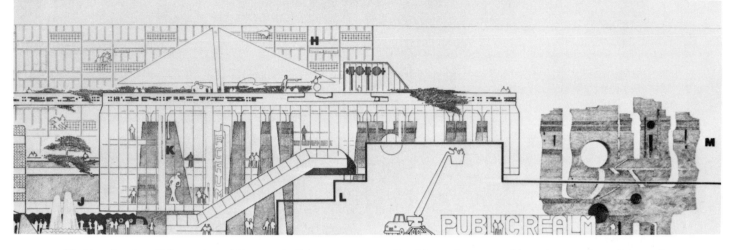

Working drawing: (J) Fountain and Courtyard off the street. (K) Interior pylons surfaced with citizens' art. (L) Line showing height limit of entrepreneur additions grouped around the Castle Sculpture (M) of an armature framework for citizens' craft and art. Themes of landforms, imagined ruins, and body and castle metaphors become reference frames accommodating passages of surface ornament and additions by local individuals. The creative professional artist, or master craftsperson, working with citizens, becomes a producer and assembler who does not violate the individual's unique work but transforms it by giving it a new and powerful context. Ruth Asawa, whose bronze San Francisco fountain is assembled from castings of bread dough figures, demonstrates that even a small lump of clay offered by a three-year-old can be transformed into a believable cloud by association with other pieces in a strong frame. All armatures do not necessarily resemble Asawa's assemblages but her system that involves professional artists and craftspersons as well as citizens promises a new future for architectural ornament.

For an armature of city scale, as numbers of involved citizens increase, opportunity for each to have any say in the final assemblage may be lessened, and consequently the artist's or architect's control increased. To keep a balance between the two, small assemblages can be brought together in larger ones and perhaps themes chosen and feedback received by television, so that ornament becomes a community expression. (*Drawing by Herb Greene.*)

Benches in the open-air Nikonmachi-Buchanan Mall, San Francisco, are designed to receive well-proportioned panels of people's art assembled by artist Ruth Asawa. Concrete supports make a simple framework accommodating individual designs and provide dignity and charm uncommon in similar settings. (*Photo by Ronald Hammer. Courtesy of San Francisco Redevelopment Agency.*)

removed from their work. To propose a theory of ornament for armatures that predicts form before the experience of producers and audience has had a chance to evolve together is a dilemma. Nevertheless, it is possible that shared ideas and consensus regarding artistic expression and preferred techniques will develop into culturally recognized canons.

In art, as in social and political patterns, possibilities in the present are conditioned by what has happened in the past. For the ornamentation of armatures I find social and aesthetic inspiration in the theories and work of Ruskin, Sullivan and Gaudi.

In the nineteenth century John Ruskin believed ornament should be applied to buildings as an expression of the populace. Making clear the social ground for ornament, it was important to him that craftsmen be unfettered by authoritarian dictates or aristocractic pretensions, and they be "happy contented workers" who sustained a living tradition of art and craftsmanship, and yet were free to express their individuality. The variety that would be the outcome of individual action he likened to the variety found in nature. Ruskin also voiced for architecture what the Romantic movement accomplished in literature. He spoke in behalf of feeling, association, memory and other poetic and aesthetic attributes of the natural world that were being dismissed by the dominant forces of mechanism which ruled science and which were to have a profound influence on Modern architecture.

As we enter the 1980's we might argue that the reductionist forms of Mies Van der Rohe—repetitive, machined and consciously unhistorical—have been accurate reflections of the dominant attitudes of the Western technological nations. However, machine production and uniform repetition are currently being questioned on both economic and aesthetic grounds. To growing numbers of economists, politicians and thinkers, automated, energy-intensive production is becoming a false god to our economic and social good health. The indifference to individuals and the regimentation implicit in Miesian architecture have been found appropriate to corporate and bureaucratic organizations but do not answer the needs of citizens who seek to participate in a more responsive environment. As long ago as 1860, Ruskin foresaw that architecture would become an "endless perspective of black skeleton and blinding square."

A generation later, architect Louis Sullivan's handling of ornament and color, and his belief that poetic expressions of hope, love, death and other glimpses of the spirit are necessary to enhance the beauty of architecture had strong affinities with Ruskin. More ideal than real, his idea was to model buildings according to a "form building force" supposedly present in organisms, even in crystals. Our most important inheritance from Sullivan is the concept of a mode that formally unifies all the diverse physical elements of architecture. Although the continuity of surface in the work of H. H. Richardson must be counted among precursors, it was Sullivan who extended these concepts in his use of ornament to an expression of imagery intended to be uniquely derived for each build-

ing and which revealed sentiments, emotions and ideas not expressible in terms of mass, structure and space alone. Sullivan's work was part of the growing trend in the nineteenth century to use shape and geometry to express formal ideas without explicit references to previous historic styles.

Darwinian evolution and other biological

Below: Ornament on the Piazza S. Marco, Venice. John Ruskin saw architecture primarily as a vehicle for painting and sculpture, in his view the proper modes of expression for the voices of humankind. One of his favorite examples is St. Mark's Cathedral, which brings together Roman, Gothic, Byzantine and Renaissance forms in a style that is more applied than integrated. Ruskin's dictum on painting and sculpture would, I believe, be an unnecessary constraint on citizen craftspersons and artists, but much of his reasoning is pertinent to armatures. It was by acts of interested workers in different periods of history that buildings, he said, were to become "geological paintings" revealing the attitudes and character of a nation. (*Photo by DEON.*)

Exterior ornament on Louis Sullivan's Guaranty Building, Buffalo, New York, 1894–5. As a revolt against architectural eclectism and inspired by biological analogies, Sullivan's articulated frame expressing window, spandrel, pier, column and entrance (under the arch and lintel) is covered with delicate relief that pulses in an image of energy and continuity. Sullivan's genius is seen in his ability to scale and pattern ornament so that it seems to grow out of the particular mass composition of which it is a part. Armatures propose a synthesis between Ruskin's expression by free craftsmen and Sullivan's giving form to an evolutionary continuity: People's individual works are connected to formal statements of historic continuum, a kind of architectural analogy to "Leaves of Grass," where each phenomenon is celebrated for its uniqueness and its derivation from the universe, and a building process by which artist-facilitators and architects tackle the problem of scaling and otherwise integrating diverse works into a poetic frame. (*Photo by Nanine Hilliard Greene.*)

theories at the same time were focusing attention on the continuity of organisms. Influenced by concepts such as growth, natural rhythms and organic plasticity which were aspects of nature, Sullivan sought to model with abstractions of shape, groupings and interwoven axes. The biological facts of growth and continuity that fascinated Sullivan and which are expressed in his ornament we would now see as important scientific details against the wider context of the physical continuum of space-time. Discoveries that relative positions are required for measurement in this continuum, and the importance of the non-homogeneous aspects of events, undermine the unconscious centrism of Sullivan's view. Like most architects today, he believed that the creativity of a single architect was sufficient to render an entire building.

Armatures, on the other hand, seek an expressive form able to incorporate the work of many different individuals, each with different values which in a sense allow different viewpoints of the same building, a form which will at the same time provide a unifying background for the interrelationships among diverse contributions. If this background is to hold together an agglomeration of very diverse objects, it must accomplish this through the creation of symbols that signify our awareness of the space-time continuum, symbols which supply the *unifying context* for castings, caryatids, mottos, or whatever participants see fit to make. However, the integral character and continuity in Sullivan's ornament still has application for us. His modulating elements synthesizing geometry with organic form suggest energy, lyricism and life process. Their plasticity is prophetic of the transformations that our present cosmology requires. Sullivan's expression of continuity and biological growth may be combined with the mind's ability to cross-classify seemingly *dis*continuous objects and meanings in terms that create continuity and maintain integrity. This idea of continuum of changing forms is beautifully expressed by Gaudi in the unfinished church of the Sagrada Familia. Through mastery of line and form, Gaudi harmonizes diverse experiences ranging from roots in the history of architecture, the life pulse of the organic world and human exaltation. We find consistent meanings amid the diverse references. Transformations in Gaudi's work exhibit perhaps the deepest intuition on record of the power of synthesizing abstractions from diverse experience into architectural form.

There is always a need to use icons to call at-

104

tention to beliefs and philosophies. The early Christians, for example, denied Roman corporeality and realistic narrative sculpture by evolving flat, suspended, yet constricted figures to direct the viewer toward an impersonal, other-worldly submission. Le Corbusier during his purist period in the 1920's favored the cube, cylinder and cone as ultimate reductions he believed were required by the mind and eye. The gradual introduction of non-Euclidean geometries and the use of them by Einstein in his astonishing work, and their subsequent popularization, has helped people more accurately to "picture" relativity involving time and space. Signs of simultaneity, chance and non-Euclidean spatial cues appropriately designed into an image become a kind of shorthand or iconography calling our attention to the extensive overlapping and non-homogeneous character of our sense awareness of space and form, much as Euclidean forms stand for spatial simplification and the values of purity, uniformity and constancy. Seeing with any sense of comprehension requires conceptual thought based on what one has come to believe, however un-

conscious such thought may have become in the process. Thus, science has made new discoveries and has influenced (and been influenced by) philosophy. Both have changed our comprehension of how the universe is organized and are making us ready for a visual aesthetic that integrates chance juxtapositions and constant change.

Another aspect of this aesthetic is that it suggests the possibility of transcending the material composing an armature. In the Middle Ages a person sought the essence of God and Divine Light in pearls, onyx and stained glass, objects with appropriately sensuous and symbolic metaphors. Even the water jugs and rugs in a Vermeer painting can lead us today to transcendence and spirit. We moderns find aesthetic values in rusted iron as well as in fine materials. Our empirical attitude compares, measures and absorbs contrasts. An armature can provide a focus, a heightening of contrasts that encourages us to understand species and kind, order, number, properties and attributes. To enhance the contemplative attitude within contexts recalling time, destiny, ecology and other cosmic

A plaster model of the Church of the Sagrada Familia, Barcelona by architect Antonio Gaudi. The lower portion of each column is designed with references to a traditional column: it is symmetrical, there are lines of entasis. As the eye travels upward, the large knuckle from which multiple members spring suggests a plant with four budlike forms that can be read as cowls with human and religious overtones. Their semi-closed position seems to be a mediate stage between the straight fluted column and the splayed open forms as they merge with the ceiling. We see the structural forces of architecture combined with biologic and anthropomorphic references. The branchlike spreading of each column in its upward thrust is like a human gesture of exaltation, a visual echo of a hallelujah chorus. *(Photo by Renato dü Four, Courtesy Amigos de Gaudi-U.S.A.)*

reference frames is to encourage our spiritual access and to sharpen our perception of the role of the material object as gateway to the spiritual. Ultimately the armature can make a statement that all physical objects are seen in terms of each other in a space-time continuum, and that every object can be related to the continuum for fuller comprehension.

In the twelfth century, the initiator of the Gothic tradition was Abbot Suger. He was deeply moved by religious artifacts encrusted with jewels, glowing stained glass windows and richly carved cloisters. Suger believed there were hierarchies of beauty in the variety of fine and coarse objects and that material beauty would lead him toward spiritual beatitude. But, by the time of his prelacy, opposition was well-formed in the Cistercian Puritanism of Bernard of Clairvaux who saw Suger's philosophy as a revolt of the temporal against the eternal, a preempting of the spirit with the senses. Records of these two luminaries show that a dialectic within the Western tradition was already well established eight hundred years ago. A rich architectural expression, drowned in material objects, was and still is, opposed to an ascetic, reductionist expression intended to facilitate the contemplation of pure ideals.

The polarities of Suger and Bernard have come down to us in twentieth century architecture. Frank Lloyd Wright with his rich palette of materials, highly articulated forms and his complex modulations of light that accept nature and the material world, descends from Suger, while Mies Van der Rohe with his restricted palette of materials and colors and his often severe rectangular buildings standing apart from nature, is closer to the beliefs of Bernard.

To obtain a width of contrasts and in recognition of the platonic attitude of Bernard, not all the walls and pavings of an armature need be covered with profuse ornament. There might be austere, restrained surfaces and forms "zoned" as permanent parts of the armature not merely plain and inert but designed in their own right to remain quiet, ascetic and free from tensions as a way of expressing the human need for rectitude and tranquility. In art images throughout history these quiet forms have ranged from the air and space of Sung landscapes to the flat backgrounds of Mondrian. While I consider the aesthetic of an armature to be in the ornamented tradition of Suger, these polarities are so deeply embedded in Western culture, I see both as necessary for expression in a building program that invites loyalty from citizens with diverse aesthetic outlooks. Utilizing vibrant ethnic colors in contrast to the reticence of whitewashed New England churches seems to me an exciting design opportunity for the armature as a ground symbolizing degrees of harmonizing of differences. Each individual piece represents a point of view, an act or a response that can be compared with others within the ground as the poetic frame that stands for a common destiny. This context calls attention to the interdependency as well as the individuality of the pieces. We can speculate on relationships against a background that both protects values and admits differences. The armature hypothesis proposes a rebirth of ornament as an accommodation of public expression more *in*clusive than any ornament known to history.

Since early in this century, many taste-makers and intellectuals have denounced ornament. This can be accounted for as a reaction to the embellishments of the royal and the rich and tasteless imitations by a growing bourgeoisie. It can also be attributed to the devaluation of meaning in historical ornament, to widespread belief in the mythic values of industrialization and the machine, and to the rise of the abstract in Modern design. Nevertheless, evidence in the third quarter of this century seems overwhelming that people still need and enjoy ornamenting, embellishing and adorning themselves and their environment. We ornament our persons with clothing, jewelry and cosmetics. We grant quality in ornament our highest interest and award it great status. Thousands will queue up to see the crown jewels of England or the intricate funerary objects from King Tut's tomb. Customized cars attest to the process of ornamentation that enables people to establish their identity. In architecture both cosmic order or temporary flashes of wit can be expressed in ornament and will help us ward off boredom and alienation.

Not only does ornament appeal to us for cul-

The restless and "unfinished" surfaces of Pablo Picasso's *Man With A Sheep* convey anxiety that reinforces the sense of uncertainty in the man's stance and expression and engages the viewer to complete his or her own meaning. Surface texture, which often plays a more symbolic role in sculpture than in architecture, can be developed for specific surfaces on armatures. Perhaps the most profound value of an art image is that it permits a recall of attitudes from earlier times within a matrix of new significance, as shown here by Picasso's subtle allusions to ideal poise from the classical tradition brought together with modern uncertainty. One can envision buildings that allow us to rediscover old assumptions and at the same time are designed to show changing feelings. (*Philadelphia Museum of Art, Given by R. Sturgis and Marion B. F. Ingersoll.*)

tural reasons but for physical and psychological ones as well. We know enough about perception to realize that the eye and mind have developed in response to the continuous shifting of visual focus and the scanning of visual detail. Visual deprivation can cause depression and bodily upset. Evidence for the value of ornament as a natural consequence of human perception is ample and even the most callous architect of today looks for some texture in materials to pleasure the eye. However, one be-

comes inured to thousands of square yards of striated concrete, endlessly repetitive curtain walls and mirror glass façades. It is obvious that contemporary building programs are sorely lacking in modes to facilitate a meaningful expression of ornament.

I suspect there are many architects, especially the younger ones, who would personally enjoy using ornament in their architectural designs but must reject the idea because of exorbitant costs. To achieve visual stimulation of a high order I am suggesting an armature frame that invites labor-intensive creative programs and that once again makes ornament on buildings a practical possibility.

The Expressive Ground

Because I place great importance on the formal expression of backgrounds for citizens' work, I have selected briefly from sculpture and painting features I believe show how backgrounds are developed to enhance important details and to become subtle reference frames. In the bronze figure, *Man With A Sheep,* Picasso shows us precise and evocative details seen in conjunction with relatively unfinished areas. The vague details of the sheep's body and the man's torso and the textures which are roughened, frayed and gouged suggest not so much a literal indication of subject or substance as an imminence from which the recognizable details of the image emerge and to which they may return. Our main purpose here is to note the intense interest and satisfaction obtained by a mixture of closures, such as frightened sheep and unstable man that are relatively clear, combined with large areas of surface and texture that are relatively ambiguous.

The need for detail to emerge from a ground that has many meanings, as in sculpture and painting, can be translated into ornament and ground in architecture. For purposes of variety and to establish contextual backgrounds, the textured areas of an armature building can be designed to bridge between details of citizen's art. These portions can have scale and color relating to their location, and forms that are made purposely vague yet suggestive of shapes that are of appropriate interest.

Above: Devonian Age fossils are exposed along the Falls of the Ohio within a half mile of downtown Louisville, Kentucky. For an armature in the Ohio Valley, reliefs made from on-site castings can be used to create textures with regional connotations of geologic age and local landforms, as well as provide interest as abstract patterns. (*Photos by Dr. Ernest M. Ellison.*)

Left: New Technologies vastly extend the range of subjects and techniques for creating architectural ornament. The illustration shows the suitability of stainless steel as a medium for chemical engraving. A photograph of spinach leaves has been used in a demonstration panel. (*Photo: Courtesy Bullock & Turner Ltd.*)

108

I am emphasizing developing the armature as a ground for the production of citizen art and craft as well as an area for creations by architects and artists. Throughout the book, a variety of symbolic forms have been suggested including visual gradations from solids to transparencies; images of layered historic or geologic strata; images that evoke metaphors of the passage of time; abrupt contrasts that denote the clash of different contexts and time sets; or forms that suggest non-Euclidean geometries. Within my limited powers, I have tried to image some of these symbols in my drawings.

The Western tradition of painting, as well as sculpture, is rich in the treatment of details emerging from a ground which supplies meaning to the details. A three-dimensional armature will offer possibilities of extending the tradition with new techniques, an enlarged pool of talents and with insights from our widening perspective of the world.

Below: Collage with a Vermeer painting and Russell Lee photograph. In my attempt to image a continuum which lets the painting and the photograph coexist across three hundred years, we see analogies without committing ourselves to the idea that the two events are equal. Although not satisfied with my solution, I believe the issue can be addressed conceptually and pictorially and that successful formulation can be applied to architectural armatures. Continua can be designed to relate to specific clusters and pieces of people's art, and people's art can be selected and integrated with existing sections of a built continuum. (*Vermeer. "The Love Letter." Amsterdam, Rijkmuseum. Photograph by Russell Lee, Farm Security Administration. Collage by Herb Greene.*)

Jan Vermeer. *Woman Holding a Balance.* The artist has rendered the shadow of the right side of the headdress as if it were a hand. The hand is larger than life and counterpoints the head in its inclination. Vague in indication, one condition for open-ended interpretation, it is explicit enough to be recognized. The shadowy hand in context with other cues, such as the beatific light and the painting of the Last Judgment on the wall, and the contemplative and wistful woman, suggests a God-like or religious intent, supportive and enveloping. Vermeer uses subtle cues to call forth harmonized meanings, perhaps on subliminal levels. In armatures, diverse and subtle images will challenge us to look more closely and, to our surprise and delight, discover details and meaning not obvious at first sight. (*Photo courtesy of the National Gallery of Art, Washington, D. C. Widener Collection.*)

Subliminal cues of terrified or sickly smiling faces are sometimes air brushed into ice cubes in magazine advertising to encourage soothing one's anxieties in liquor. The eye is capable of processing about 50,000 bits of information per second, much of it on unconscious levels. In imaging the "ground" in the armatures, both subliminal and subtle cues have important implications. Cues whose meanings harmonize with prominent features amid the armature details or ornament may be developed; cues that signify the idea of the continuum itself can be implanted; and cues that provide vivid contrast to the armature and to the ornament are all possible. Instead of negative and coercive subliminal cues, armatures will employ positive signs and symbols. (*Drawing by Herb Greene.*)

Armature with sloping piers. Intended to catch the viewer off balance, to pique curiosity and invite closer inspection, this armature forces an interaction with passersby. The sloping piers offer niches where pedestrians can stop for conversation as well as a strong visual ground for the accumulated details of citizens' art that flows across the paving and up the piers themselves. The color and the scale of the horizontal bands would set rules for citizen ornament. In an armature whose program is avowedly to increase awareness and elicit a complex response, the drawing shows a rhythmic progression of windows whose irregularities suggest children's drawings and which produce an illusion of animation in contrast to the static, massive wall. The irregular voids with faint analogies to eyes and face offer opportunities for playful empathy. The sloping piers gradually emerge from the building to mark the entrance with an elephantine thickness and gait. Together these sets of cues encourage the viewer to overlap references to the solidity of historic masonry architecture and "rational" building with projections of character and humor. Perhaps everyone won't see or appreciate such half-hidden cues but they can be available for an increasingly literate public. (*Drawing by Herb Greene.*)

8 Collage and Surrealism in Designing Armatures

A collage of ages, a collage of skins, a collage of tastes—folks carrying vegetables and tourists browsing in boutiques elbow to elbow. Even more exciting are the people working on crafts tonight in a great curving, glass-enclosed section of the armature, a crystal palace envelope that protects an interior of piers, pylons and cantilevered floors covered with people's arts, a combination of a bazaar, a hanging garden and a miniature roofscape from Chambord. Without the need to build weather-tight roofs, additions to the interior structure have taken ingenious, fanciful and surrealist forms. Crossing to the opposite side of the square where vines cover large unfinished portions of the armature wall, I see leaves ripple in the wind. Nostalgia and premonition—I wonder what it might become.

COLLAGE has possibly become the most common mode of composition in the visual arts. If we think of painting, sculpture, advertising and film we note the explosive development of collage. While collage has been used sparingly by architects I see it as a necessary technique for designers of armatures. Not only would architects have to respond to existing buildings by incorporating or collaging them into armatures but architects would be called

on to make appropriate frameworks to accommodate the works of various citizen crafts groups, architectural fragments and other unpredictable situations for physical design. The architect would also work with facilitators and craftspersons to determine rules for harmonizing diverse works. In this chapter I present a brief theoretical discussion of collage and give a few examples of how it might be employed by architects.

Obviously, techniques for ornamenting armatures and adding spaces to them would not be limited to collage. Builders and designers would utilize other techniques and undoubtedly invent new ones. But collage is fundamental to armatures. While there have been architectures in the past made up of additions and subtractions before collage became an art form, it is difficult to imagine present-day armatures without an understanding of collage in its most relevant usages.

The word collage has its roots in the French word "bricolage" used in games and sports in reference to accidental or extraneous movement or avoidance. It came to mean someone using his hands with unorthodox means to make things when compared with traditional artisanship. It was in France during the last half of

At the turn of this century, some architects made surprising combinations of historic styles. Bernard Maybeck in his 1907 First Church of Christ Scientist, Berkeley, California, employed hollow concrete columns with Romanesque capitals, beams decorated with Gothic inspired tracery, Byzantine color surfaces, Japanese framing and banks of industrial factory windows. Maybeck's freewheeling assemblage and his ability to give his designs formal order anticipate work in a collage style. (*Photos by Nanine Hilliard Greene.*)

Armature with reconstituted façades. A collage of historic façades as a frame for citizen art. Cherished structures lost to urban renewal, fire and other causes can be reconstituted to modulate new high-rise structures with the ground and to integrate them into the historic city. Important cues of lost buildings, and actual fragments can be used to create an architecture of pedestrian scale with ornament at street level, individual entrances, meeting places directly off the sidewalk and elevators to roof gardens. An archaeological approach can recreate images of a particular building, block or district. (*Drawing by Herb Greene.*)

the nineteenth century that collage was used to force an aesthetic contemplation of manufactured objects. In sculpture in 1880, Degas fixed an actual cloth tutu on a bronze ballerina. The realism and fragility of cloth against the bronze figure with its classical associations of the timeless and the ideal shocked the viewing public.

Today any artistic composition of disparate materials and objects held together with unifying colors or lines is called a collage. This usual meaning is not sufficiently wide to include all the uses that collage has come to signify. The principles of collage have been applied in various media. In sculpture, the term assemblage is used to denote constructions that include

Below: A section of the armature as exhibition hall or civic center on a rectangular block. Overlapping time frames are suggested by the inclusion of historic buildings with the encrusted base reminiscent of archaeological layers against the high technology roof structure. In designing loose-fit frameworks for armatures architects may provide a collage of cues: a heavy, rough, earthy component and, in contrast, the smoothness, transparency and weightlessness that can be obtained by new technologies.

The courtyard under the roof membrane can be cooled by recirculated water flowing over its exterior surface. Qualities of old and new, massiveness and lightness, warmth and coolness afforded by these contrasts are capable of harmonizing most additions. (*Drawing by Herb Greene.*)

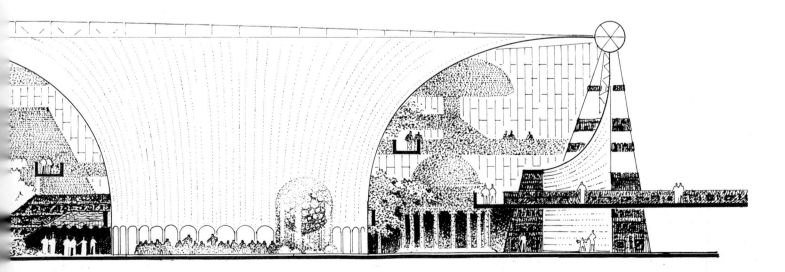

Madison Civic Center, Madison, Wisconsin. Hardy Holzman Pfeiffer Associates, architects. Portions of a 1928 theater are incorporated into the Center. Stepped-up windows in new walls build up to a salvaged Spanish Renaissance entrance façade. In another project, the Mt. Healthy School near Columbus, Indiana, the architects combined two kinds of new façades for the "front" and "back" of the school, using different brick and window designs. Inside, the colors and materials of teaching modules, lockers, cabinets and floors, derived from the environment of subdivision houses familiar to the students, are juxtaposed with bar joist ceilings and masonry walls of contemporary schoolhouse vernacular. The firm is also noted for plan compositions which express a collage attitude toward program components. (*Photos by Norman McGrath.*)

found or ready-made objects. In film, montage denotes significant combinations of diverse events seen in individual frames that are either merged literally in a new frame or that appear in consecutive or closely-spaced frames so that new meaning is created by the collision of combined elements. I am including assemblage and montage under the heading of collage.

In a collage the original or found object provides a sense of the immediate and unexpected by utilizing an object at hand rather than a crafted or manufactured object designed for the job. Features of the found object and its associated meanings remain as indications of a world wider than one narrowed by the aesthetic and logical homogeneity of the new construction. A sharp sense of the past colliding with the present can be a result. The found object also stands for a world that is beyond alteration by the subjectivity of the designer and can contribute to aesthetic distance—a detachment from self that is a valued component of aesthetic experience. The found object also contributes already developed meaning out of which the designer can explore new ideas and qualities.

I also use the term collage to refer to the combining of people's art (which in itself may be collage) with the long-lived symbolic frame of armatures; and to the social process which will allow individuals and groups, often of different ethnic and ideological backgrounds, to come together in unexpected combinations.

The import of collage lies in the harmonious utilization of aspects of physical objects in unfamiliar contexts in order to make new meaning, and the ability of the original objects to retain their efficacy as signs of their original situation. The often surprisingly affective meanings and feelings that may be evoked by their integration into an unfamiliar context are characteristic of collage.

One of the most powerful and fascinating works of collage is Picasso's *Baboon and Young*. The head of the mother is fashioned from a toy automobile and her upper body out of a pot-bellied stove. The idea of a toy car being the head of a baboon is made plausible and arresting by the addition of out-sized ears. The front fender of the car imparts a grin or leer to the face. In contrast, the division between radiator grille and bumper has been fashioned into a closed mouth. The round head of one baby is purposefully shaped. It could be a human head and its longish arms are of a creature as human as it is apelike. The clinging, outstretched arms, for instance, can be taken as a symbol of humankind propitiating the frontally staring car which, among other possibilities, can be read as an icon of the machine age. Thoughts and feelings engendered by recognition of these features seem haunting and paradoxical.

My analysis may give the impression that the process involves a linear interpretation of individual cues. This is not the case. It is much more like a circular dialectic with random and simultaneous cues being evaluated on both conscious and subconscious levels. The mind is comparing shape, number, color, form, texture and stored knowledge as a basis to intensify and control the transfer between toy car and baboon mother to call attention to likenesses, and to narrow down alternatives. We make new meaning out of analogies between forms not usually associated with each other. By making associations, displacements and new combinations we create symbols that unify the dissimilar at a level of deep feeling or highly interesting intellectual significance.

The need to find the image that unifies disparate objects at some unconscious level of the mind calls for a keen understanding of harmonies and disharmonies. Some designers are committed to a position that ignores harmony. They present collections of random events. Others advocate combining industrial products in ways for which they were not intended, enabling individuals to exercise creativity in the face of a coercive commercial world. In my opinion the need for harmony in collage is not circumvented by current strategies or attitudes of designers. Aesthetic value lies in the harmonious inclusion of diversity in a single expression as in the *Baboon and Young* in which objects attached to deeply harmonized experience are brought together to become provocative. Mother and young, prayer and machine, the comic and the obeisant, are harmonized.

Unfortunately, many architectural situations calling for collage and affected by contemporary technological and aesthetic trends have mini-

Baboon and Young, 1951, by Pablo Picasso. The flat-footed baboon mother with her ambiguous clinging offspring and vague expressionist hands, which do not so much support the infants as extend into space, restructure our expectations and invite us to make new meanings. In an armature way of building, the aesthetic energy that can be obtained by a diversity of unpredictable combinations and additions can be optimized. I believe this energy waits on the understanding of a building as we would the *objet trouvé*. By this I mean the associations set up by the object are stimuli to new combinations of ideas. Painting, sculpture, literature and film show masterworks of collage that depend on this understanding. Architecture, a more unwieldy art, has yet to realize the potential (*Collection, The Museum of Modern Art, New York, Mrs. Simon Guggenheim Fund.*)

Düsseldorf. Project for a new artificial ground layer by Wimmenauer, Szabo, Kasper and Meyer, 1969. Many avant-garde architects in the sixties would have introduced huge monoarchitectures into cities without consideration for fine tuning with existing urban fabric. (*Photomontage by Foto Lipecki.*)

mized, ignored or misconstrued the requirements of harmony. In a proposal for Düsseldorf, for instance, architects proposed a layering of decks above neo-Renaissance buildings. Although these glassy cylinders provide an element harmonizing with the regularity of windows and pilasters below, this harmony is minor when we realize these continuous tubes would have spread out over the entire city. It is difficult to imagine such a network of giant passageways framing the varied roofs and spires of the historic skyline.

In the drawing of an office building overstriding a small chapel in Athens, a situation of smaller scale than the Düsseldorf proposal indicates a similar outcome, which is to treat the collision of unrelated artifacts as sheer juxtaposition without effort at accommodation at a deeper level of meaning. This position can have complex roots. It may be a product of a classicism that has always minimized context,

Office built over a chapel in Athens, Greece. Merely saving the chapel can be considered a victory, but collision without accommodation can produce negative social implications. (*Sketch by Herb Greene.*)

116

or may represent a determinist interpretation of functionalism, or be a response to movements that celebrate a machine aesthetic and tenets of anti-art, or simply be an expedient architectural response to sentiment to retain the chapel. At best this procedure acknowledges the individuality of each structure with its separate *raison d'être*, but wit, deeper poetry or a civilizing sense of caring about how one might accommodate the artifacts, is foregone.

In architecture, the aesthetic consequences of collage are sobering, as well as exciting. Successful expression will not be realized through recognition of technological and social forces. These will only produce a proliferation of heterogeneous forms. Arguing that the scale and functional requirements of large urban facilities like rapid transit lines and the prerogatives of free enterprise make artistic harmony in cities impractical only demonstrates the need for mediating architectural features. There is the potential within armatures to provide an architectural form that carries poetic values and has the capacity to harmonize colliding additions.

About the same time artists were developing collage, 1915 to 1925, the philosopher, Alfred North Whitehead was offering an interpretation of our knowledge and perception of physical matter that could explain the effectiveness of collage and show that its rationale is built into the structure of the world. Because our intellectual heritage and our interpretations of perception are usually based on Newtonian-Cartesian concepts—that nature divides matter into uniform, predictable, self-contained bodies—it continues to be difficult for us to accept that all objects are physically and perceptually extended from one another, an idea fundamental to our discovery of order in Picasso's *Baboon and Young*. Whitehead presented a view that integrated contemporary physics with perception. Planets, rocks, pieces of furniture, a human brain and "empty" space which appear to us as separate things, are all modifications of the same field that exhibits different arrangements of relatively few types of atomic particles. The particles exhibit properties of migration and transformation so that the field is in a state of flux. To Whitehead, perception involves the functioning of the body with its complex sense receptors and capacity for information storage and recall as it responds to activities in the field. During perception one is aware, for example, of a cup on one's desk. Perception might involve the cognizance of the circular rim, a highlight on the surface, a textural quality, a particular color or our recognition of the flatness of the desk. These recognizable characteristics or features enter into our experience by way of memory. We recognize them from our recall of other situations which we have experienced. It takes time to perceive features while their physical situations extend around us as the medium we live through. However, physical situations last only an instant because matter is always in a state of fluctuation. Thus recognition of features from memory acknowledges our experience or imagination of the connections among situations within different parts of the field that Whitehead calls the continuum of space-time. He shows how any feature is capable of occurring in any physical situation within the space-time continuum because its occurrence, seemingly incompatible at one position in the continuum, can become consistent at another. However, this does not mean that all occurrences are equally interesting, for interest is determined by the experience and bias of the observer.

I believe many people think of collage with intellectual misgivings as though its combinations were based on accident, or as if the difficulties of fashioning harmonious combinations indicated a violation of some fundamental order. Rather, the consistencies of collage are the result of our memory as creatures in the physical field. Although Whitehead stresses there is no rigorous system for analyzing physical situations and their remembered features with precise determination, we have come to see material things as interconnected and their forms as being able to commingle.

Collage is a natural and decisive outcome of Western art and philosophy and not an accident of composition to be limited to humorous combinations or ad hoc utilitarianism. Although now so popular as to be a staple of grade school art classes and hobby shop kits, we need not deceive ourselves about the ease of applying it to architecture and urban design where ques-

Max Ernst. *La Ville Petrifieé.* The encroaching jungle and a city deserted or decayed, archetypal symbols of the unconscious, gain fascination in Ernst's warmly colored and intricately rendered dream. Streaming horizontals suggest the passage of time. These archetypes could be developed in armatures and gardens for armatures. Like the most aesthetically successful of Ernst's mysterious forests and ruins, armatures will aspire to the charms of color and texture and to the power of formal organization to convey symbols. (*Photo: Courtesy City Art Gallery, Manchester, England.* © *Estate of Max Ernst 1980.*)

tions of scale, function, permanence and public acceptance are paramount. Yet there is a growing awareness that collage offers the most promising urban design strategy for dealing with technological and social pluralism. Its design techniques and opportunities can gear us to accomodate diverse historical styles and to unify disparate works of citizens' art. Once our idea of order extends beyond restrictions of uniformity, predictability and self-contained physical forms, the designer and public can accept the wide range of aesthetic possibilities suggested by a long-lasting armature with its heterogeneous additions.

Picasso, in *Baboon and Young* and earlier works, found that he and the Western tradition were producing a restructuring of things we perceive through the multiple spatial situations of cubism. Cubism, a new synthesis to which Picasso made important contributions about 1908–1920, represented a new function not explicitly recognized in European painting which up to that time had presupposed a single point of view and a figure or object in a single location. The theory of multiple perspectives in cubism relates to Whitehead's theory of time. It was his view that multiple perspectives, each with its individual way of involving itself in the world, are required during the integration that constitutes our response to the various features of a physical situation. Time, which is locked into individual perspectives of each feature enters into the concreteness of the physical thing before us.

One building that incorporates the cubist mode is Le Corbusier's Notre Dame du Haut which we have talked about before but would now like to look at as an example of cubism in architecture. At Ronchamp, more than fifty years after the appearance of Cubism in European art, Le Corbusier has utilized cubist strategies to compose very different forms to convey multiple perspectives. Arresting and fresh, the façades are different on all four sides as if to present several "selves" in the same building. The roof, almost overwhelming in its visibility on the approach side, is expressed not at all on the opposite side. Le Corbusier has invested the building with simultaneous meanings derived from our experience of historical times—a building with a great roof; a building with a great wall. The cubist method of representing an object as it might be at different moments in time and space can be used as a strategy to deal with the colliding diversities in armatures. And the incorporation of cues of overlapping historical time frames will, I believe, lead us inevitably into the cubist philosophy.

An urban square as armature. This sketch, barely more than a cartoon, shows an intricate, colorful tapestry of people's work that covers the paving and runs up the walls of an armature. Like the Max Ernst painting it suggests the use of compatible uniformities such as color, texture, and topology by which we lift out the notion of harmony and subsume the notion of diversity. (*Drawing by Herb Greene.*)

Detail of an armature wall with people's art. Collaged against a frame of horizontal structural members, which can allude to a time stream or to geological strata, are diverse designs made by citizens and composed by architect-artist facilitators. (*Drawing by Herb Greene.*)

Notre Dame du Haut, Ronchamp, France. Le Corbusier, architect. Ronchamp can be understood as a cubist collage of created forms designed with references to history, rather than "found" forms. Towers shaped a bit like nuns' coifs or like towers seen in Mediterranean cultures suggest religious and anthropomorphic references. They merge with heavy walls and yet are separated by decisive vertical joints. The roof, barely visible at far left is cut off as if by a sharp plane. Le Corbusier has subtly utilized the cutting planes and congruent edges of cubism to articulate diverse forms. (*Photo by Ezra Stoller. ©ESTO.*)

Surrealism is another movement concerned with memory which has had a powerful influence on the arts but very little on architecture. In the early twenties, at the same time that the rational reductionism of the International style, supported by the machine production of standardized members, was increasing its hold on architecture, the fantasies and dreams of the recently discovered unconscious were dictating surrealist philosophy.

Surrealism, a literary and artistic movement launched in 1924 by the French poet, André Breton, proclaimed that all artistic, social, scientific and philosophical values are radically transformed through total liberation of the unconscious. While many people have been repelled by some surrealist works which show disintegration, decay, sadism and the persistently unwholesome, others see positive aspects in the surrealist legacy. Certainly the plastic arts, literature, film and even the recent worldwide popularity of the Muppet television show, acknowledge to some degree an acceptance of surreal canons. The Muppets, with foam rubber monsters (some of which relate back to archaic demons) and bizarre juxtapositions of animals, vegetables, minerals and people, have become a symbol of lost inhibitions and craziness within the limits of mass acceptance. If the Muppets' deviations from ra-

Antonio Gaudi's Casa Batllo, Barcelona, 1905–1907, antedated the mainstream surrealist movement. Here Gaudi remodeled a conventional apartment building into an image of deified nature. The surface of the original building is transformed into a vision of water flecked with flowers and water lilies. Strange masks intrude in the balcony railings and the rhythmic, scaley roof is like a dragon. Gaudi's transformation reaches to the interior spaces as well as the exterior form and suggests how a collective imagination might transform an existing building into an armature. (*Photo by Ampliaciones y Reproduciones MAS, Barcelona. Courtesy Amigos de Gaudi'-Barcelona.*)

Lucien Kroll's functioning ductwork in the restaurant of the University of Louvain, Brussels, combines references to sending, receiving, looking and nuzzling with biological animation to transform the mechanical into the amusingly surreal. (*Courtesy Atelier Lucien Kroll, architect, Bruxelles.*)

tionality and frequent appetite for spontaneous associations do not owe something to widespread surrealist fallout, their fantasy must at least be seen as a verification of age-old necessities that produce similar results.

A primary belief of contemporary rationalist designers is that modern man is fundamentally different from his ancestors and needs a new environment, free from atavism, ambiguity and the irrational. On the other hand, anthropologists now see little differences between the Cro-Magnon and contemporary mind, particularly concerning the reflexes of the oldest part of the brain, the limbic system. Until the Enlightenment, men realized that both the real and the surreal are required to mediate the world. Frustrated by the limits of a one-sidedly rationalist perception, modern man may need assurance of realities beyond reason even more than his supposedly primitive forebears.

The features of surrealism which I see as most central to the issues of armatures and which are most susceptible to broad public acceptance, are the reconciliation of dream and reality, the liberation of human desires, the feeling that there is a secret and invisible side to everyday phenomena and the energy and poetry in spontaneous associations. Additionally, surrealist concerns with great cosmic symbols—sky,

earth, water—and the nostalgia for archaic forms of existence overlap with those metaphors of nature that root us to our biological and historic past and which are potentially vital references for armatures. While the predominant intention of many Surrealists was to be hallucinatory, convulsive and baffling, certain works by historically labelled Surrealists (for instance Max Ernst in his painting of gorgeously intricate forests and ruined cities and Matta with his colorful and original handling of non-Euclidean space which seems to include the psyche), are intense orchestrations of perceptions to which we can return more than once for suggestion.

To inject a measure of the hallucinatory and baffling into architecture, I have used a painting by Muzika as inspiration for a symbolic form within the courtyard of an armature. As the centerpiece in an urban open space sur-

Der Grosse Elsinor XI by František Muzika. The castle is a recurring surrealist theme. Its poetic value is that it stands for the fear of a return to the powers of the past and suggests the difficulties and perils each individual may face in a path toward the light. We are caught in both nostalgia and fear of the archaic form. (*Reproduced by permission of Mrs. Anna Muzikova. From the collection of Dr. Hans Gerling, Köln, Germany.*)

Pasadena, California. Tournament of Roses parade. The castle as recurring archetype in culture today appears on wheels. Temporary additions to armatures for festivals can result in saturation of color and a light fantasy that can contrast with more profound and long-lasting expressions. (*Photo courtesy of Pasadena Tournament of Roses.*)

rounded by indeterminate commercial structures, the ruined castle is conceived as public ornament of psychic import in contrast to the expedient and rational buildings that will probably surround it. A recurring claim is that the modern world has suppressed the irrational and eradicated the idea of chance or the intervention of fate, and in so doing has eroded the subjective and the passionate. The armature provides an outlet for expression of these feelings. The creation of this kind of public building and ornament with its potential for substance and meaning could lessen the alienation produced by architecture with its cheap and formulaic decoration which is getting all the more so in a time of inflated costs and declining craftsmanship.

Cubism and surrealism are movements that profoundly influenced twentieth century art because they presented fundamentally new and valid ideas in structure and content. Mainstream architecture—costly, relatively cumbersome and necessarily practical—has yet to develop the potentials learned from these movements. The opportunity to use this aesthetic and philosophic inheritance can come through an armature way of building with its program of longevity, creative intentions and sheltered economics. At the same time that armatures conserve historic form they can also be a vehicle for community experiments in new aesthetics. E. H. Gombrich has said that, "No lesson of psychology is perhaps more important than the multiplicity of layers, the peaceful coexistence in man of incompatible attitudes. There never was a primitive stage of man when all was magic. There never happened an evolution which wiped out the earlier phase. What happens is rather that different institutions and different situations favor and bring out a different approach to which both the artist and his public learn to respond. But beneath these new attitudes, or mental sets, the old ones survive and come to the surface in play or earnest."

Among their other roles, armatures can express the peaceful coexistence in human beings of incompatible attitudes.

I have presented armatures as a public celebration of the past and as a testament of hope for the future. They can be generators of festivity, visions and dreams. Ultimately they can provide a much needed source of fantasy, not the careful, limited fantasy put out by select professionals for mass consumption but fantasy that gives expression to our deepest intuitions, myths and incompatible attitudes. At a time when society needs new instruments to express the whole spectrum of the psyche as well as the inevitable contradictions of life in a context that strengthens human dignity, the aesthetic development of surrealism latent in armatures is a vital potential.

I do think there is originality to the idea of armatures and I believe it has important aesthetic and social implications. But in today's world, organizing social, political and economic systems for building an armature is a more formidable challenge than presenting the idea. Those who can confront and master this challenge will be real pioneers.

In this book I have contended that our present system of building produces structures with neither stability and permanence nor open-endedness and adaptability. Certainly we construct steel and reinforced concrete buildings that may last, but few of these have qualities that attract loyalties for centuries. Glass boxes, brick veneer, plastic panels and indifferent workmanship are producing, for the most part, flimsiness and ennui. The accumulation of the insubstantial in our cities and in suburbia creates a sense of no-place without even the freedom to adapt which we should be able to exercise.

The armature idea tries to encourage the building process to move two ways: toward a heavier, more long-lasting, symbolic frame and at the same time toward lighter additions and ornament by citizens and artists. Together these could form a new basis for design, rich in social and aesthetic diversity, an integration of architecture, craft and art.

Notes

The page numbers and the subject matters in parentheses refer to the pages and paragraphs where the corresponding source material is used.

Chapter 1
AN ARMATURE WAY OF BUILDING

page 11 (respect its surroundings) When I say a project interrupts the fabric of the city I am referring to the new convention-shopping-and-entertainment centers in the core of cities across America that dwarf their surroundings and disregard the existing pattern of streets. It is almost as if these new centers have dropped from another planet. Rather than form an active, people-oriented street at their perimeter, they present blank walls and parking garages. In impression and reality they are fortress-like barriers against contamination from the often aged and run-down urban environments in which they are built. Rather than encouraging physical mingling with existing shops and city activities, these centers shut themselves in and control who can enter the complex at fixed points. Such facilities with their Muzak, constant temperatures, and inward orientations may as well be located at airports as they exclude the existing city.

page 14 (the dream) Wylie Sypher, *Literature and Technology* (Random House, New York, 1968), page 191.

page 16 (streets as potential armatures) For an article on revitalizing the street as a community resource subject to its own financial and physical considerations, see Peter Wolf, "Rethinking the Urban Street: Its Economic Context" in *On Streets*. Edited by Stanford Anderson. (MIT Press, Cambridge, Mass. 1978). Pages 377–92.

page 18 (social order) Murray Edel-man, "Space and the Social Order," *Journal of Architectural Education* (JAE) Vol. XXXII, No. 2, Nov. 1978, illustrates how buildings tell us whether we are upper dogs or underdogs. In the book, *The Signature of Power, Buildings, Communication and Policy* by Harold D. Lasswell with the collaboration of Merritt B. Fox (Transaction Books, New Brunswick, New Jersey, 1979), the Introduction, in particular, reviews the relationship between environmental design and political power.

Chapter 2
THE ARCHITECT'S ROLE

page 19 ("home again") *The Unforeseen Wilderness*. Text by Wendell Berry and photographs by Gene Meatyard. (University Press of Kentucky, Lexington, 1971), page 56.

page 20 (designers and citizens) Among many publications on environmental decision-making, a useful one is the *Journal of Architectural Education* (JAE) Vol. XXXIII, No. 1, September (1979). The entire issue is on decision-making games with reference lists to other articles and books. "Take Part" refers to Lawrence Halprin and Jim Burns, *Taking Part: A Workshop Approach to Collective Creativity* (MIT Press, Cambridge, 1974).

For information on educational programs that involve architects, planners and citizens, especially young people in the U.S. and England, three sources are: The Town and Country Planning Association, 17 Carlton House Terrace, London SW1Y 5AS, England and their publication *BEE, The Bulletin of Environmental Education;* The Center for City Building Educational Programs, 2210 Wilshire Blvd., Suite 303, Santa Monica, California 90403, and their *Manual for The City Building Education Program, Architectural Consultant Edition;* and the Center for Human Environments, Graduate School of City University of New York, 33 West 42nd Street, New York, N.Y. 10036 and their *Childhood-City Newsletter.*

page 21 (architect . . . as producer) A valuable analysis of the designer in relationship to the community is Su Braden, *Artists and People* (Routledge and Kegan Paul, Ltd., London), pages 128 ff, "The Artist as Producer."

page 23 (George Emslie) In a letter April 1979, Prof. Kenneth W. Severens of the College of Charleston (S.C.) writes:

"To my knowledge, no drawing survives of Sullivan's elevation with three arches. Elmslie's account recorded in a letter to Lewis Mumford in 1931 is the usually cited explanation for the differing elevations:

'When [Sullivan] returned from Owatonna he had some, palm-of-the-hand, sketches of requirements and a study for the design. His design embodied three arches on each of the two fronts. I suggested a great 36' arch instead of the three. The building was so built.'

"However, in 1909 Elmslie had made an even more convincing claim in a letter addressed to Carl Bennett, the vice president of the Owatonna bank:

'Even the big arched windows was first thought out by me. He came back from Owatonna with a scheme for 3 arches.' "

page 25 ("ruin") For a discussion of how architects have incorporated the images of ruins, see *David Bell, "Unity and Aesthetics of Incompletion in Architecture," Architectural Design,* Vol. 49. No. 7, (1979), pages 175 ff.

Chapter 3
TOWARD SYMBOLIC ROOTS

page 30 (John Ruskin) This poetic passage is from E. P. Cook and Alexander Wedderburn, editors, *The Works of John Ruskin.* (George Allen, London. Longman Green, New York, 1903). Volume VIII, pages 233–34, paragraph 10.

page 33 ("persistence of place") Rene´ Dubos, *A God Within* (Scribner, New York, 1972), page 134.

page 34 ("the mythical past") Ernst Cassirer, *The Philosophy of Symbolic Forms* (Yale, 1955), Vol. 2; "Mythical Thought," page 105.

page 36 (monastic planning) Sherban Cantacuzino, *New Uses for Old Buildings* (Whitney Library of Design, New York, 1975), page 10.

page 44 (play as public expression) Richard Sennett, *The Fall of Public Man* (Alfred A. Knopf, New York, 1977). Chapter 11, "The End of Public Culture," pages 259 ff.

page 45 (the public realm relates and separates us) Hannah Arendt, *The Human Condition* (University of Chicago Press, Chicago, 1958), "The Public and the Private Realm," page 52.

Chapter 4
TRAGEDY AND HUMOR IN ARMATURES

pages 51 and 52 (humor as criticism) James Feibleman, *In Praise of Comedy* (Horizon Press, New York, 1970), pages 266–67.

page 57 (the element of shock) Allegra Stewart, *Gertrude Stein and the Present* (Harvard University Press, Cambridge, Mass., 1967), pages 95–96.

page 58 (scientific findings as decrees of fate) A. N. Whitehead, *Science and the Modern World* (Cambridge University Press, 1953).

Chapter 5
CREATIVE INCONVENIENCE

page 70 (greenhouses, gardens and orchards) On nature as a preferred setting see Rachel Kaplan, "The Green Experience," in Stephen and Rachel Kaplan, Editors, *Humanscape: Environments For People.* (Duxbury Press, North Scituate, Mass., 1978), pages 186 ff.

page 71 (a heavy walled house) Christopher Alexander has postulated a "thick wall house" in which the resident takes up the thick shell of the house with all its transmission of history and cultural continuity, and is able to modify it with his or her own niches and openings so that they become part of the historical process. A similar psychology is intended with the habitable elements of the armature. Christopher Alexander, "Thick Wall Pattern." *Architectural Design,* (July 1968), Volume 38, pages 324–26. Also, for a proposal that anticipates the concept of a housing armature see Ian Athfield's winning concept for an international design competition, a self-help project for a low-income district of Manila that calls for a continuous line of structures forming the boundary of the community. These structures house cooperatives, energy centers and small industries and are designed to accommodate roof gardens and building additions by users. See *Designscape,* No. 84, (September 1976), published by the New Zealand Industrial Design Council.

page 72 (urban transformations by additions) Rodrigo Perez de Arce, "Urban Transformations and the Architecture of Additions," *Architectural Design* (April 1978), page 237 ff.

page 73 (Christopher Alexander and colleagues' methods) Christopher Alexander, *A Pattern Language* (Oxford University Press, New York, 1977).

Chapter 6.
ARCHITECTURE AS A "RESPONSIBLY LIMITED TOOL."

page 82 ("responsibly limited tools") Ivan Illich, *Tools for Conviviality* (Harper & Row, New York, 1973). Page xi.

page 82 (the juiceless tomato) "Tomato Technology" by William H. Friedlander and Amy Barton, *Society* (Sept./Oct. 1976).

page 83 (mass-produced food) Wendell Berry, *The Unsettling of America: Culture and Agriculture* (Avon Books, Hearst Corporation, New York, 1978. Published by arrangement with Sierra Club Books, San Francisco, CA 94108).

page 85 ("creative work and useful action") Eric Hoffer, *The True Believer: Thoughts on the Nature of Mass Movements* (Harper and Brothers, New York, 1951). Page 51, paragraph 51, "The Bored."

pages 85 and 86 (mediating groups) Peter L. Berger and Richard John Neuhaus, *To Empower People. The Role of Mediating Structures in Public Policy* (American Enterprise Institute for Public Policy Research, Washington, D.C., 1977). A thin paperback that suggests ways to return certain kinds of decision-making to small organizations such as the family, the neighborhood, the church, labor union, etc.

page 86 (small projects capture imagination) Christopher Alexander, *The Oregon Experiment* (Oxford University Press, New York, 1975), page 65.

page 87 (the arts and crafts movement) John B. Jackson, "Craftsman Style and Technostyle," *Ornament VIA III.* (Graduate School of Fine Arts, University of Pennsylvania, 1977).

Wolfgang Pehnt, *Expressionist Architecture* (Praeger, New York, 1973). Ch. 7. "The Early Bauhaus."

page 88 (the difference between labor and work) Hannah Arendt, *The Human Condition* (University of Chicago Press, Chicago, 1958), pages 136 ff.

page 88 (public-private funding) Syndicated columnist Neal Peirce observes (December 1979) the growth of public-private partnerships for renewing cities. He cites advantages and disadvantages, the latter the potential for misuse of authority and funds, but foresees that government will be forced to use increasingly scarce public dollars to "leverage" private sector investment. After citing projects like Seattle's Freeway Park, Pioneer Square and the $60 million Westlake Mall that incorporates the relocated Seattle Art Museum, Peirce holds that city hall partnerships with neighborhoods may be the most important. To hold down taxes, neighborhoods may contract to provide local services from trash collection to street cleaning and social services, particularly recreation.

pages 89–90 (the 1930s Federal Art Project) Richard D. McKenzie, *The New Deal for Artists* (Princeton University Press, 1973).

pages 90–91 ("people working together") *Ruth Asawa's San Francisco Fountain.* By Sally B. Woodbridge, page 5. (Distributed by Hyatt House, San Francisco, CA).

page 91 (the Cambridge, Mass. Arts Fund Ordinance) City of Cambridge, Mass. Article XXIX. The Public Development Arts Fund Ordinance (1979) states that: "Art to be funded from the Public Development Arts Fund [are] projects [that] may be an 'integral part' of a building, attached to a building, placed within or outside of a building, or in the case of performing arts performed in a public building or space; said art may include but shall not be limited to paintings, sculpture, engravings, carvings, frescoes, mobiles, murals, collages, mosaics, bas-reliefs, tapestries, photographs, drawings, drama, instrumental or vocal music, dance, and landscape items, including the artistic placement of natural materials or man-made fountains or objects or other functional art objects."

page 93 (Grant's Tomb bench) Centennial Plaza Project. *The Westsider*, (New York), March 29, 1973.

page 93 (Patchwork Plaza) Cityarts, Inc. City of New York. (Parks, Recreation and Cultural Affairs Administration, 830 Fifth Avenue, New York, N.Y. 10021).

page 95 (Wall of Respect) *Guide to Chicago's Murals.* Chicago Council on Fine Arts. Introduction by Victor A. Sorell, Chairperson. (Department of Art, Chicago State University, 1978), pages 32–33.

page 95 (Corridart torn down) *The New York Times,* July 17, 1976.

page 95 (the Craigmillar Festival) Su Braden, *Artists and People,* (Routledge and Kegan Paul, Ltd., London), pages 29–37.

page 96 (amateur builders) In talking with William P. Bruder, architect in Phoenix, Arizona, I learned that he recently had sixty clients, most without construction experience,

all involved in owner-constructed additions to their houses worth up to $500,000. Bruder, who specializes in service to do-it-yourself builders has found that novices soon develop building skills and that many clients make further elaborations and additions for the sake of exercising and increasing their proficiency.

Chapter 7.
ARCHITECTURAL ORNAMENT IN A NEW CONTEXT

page 101 (ornament as grammatical expression) Sir John Summerson, "What is Ornament and What is Not" in *Ornament. VIA III.* (Graduate School of Fine Arts, University of Pennsylvania, 1977).

page 102 (John Ruskin) In his book, *Ruskin Today,* Kenneth Clark gives good reasons for the sudden fall of Ruskin's reputation and equally good reasons for the continuing value of his work. Kenneth Clark, *Ruskin Today* (Holt, Rinehart & Winston, New York, 1964).

page 103 (Ruskin's "endless perspective") Kristine O. Garrigan, *Ruskin on Architecture, His Thought and Influence* (University of Wisconsin Press, Madison, Wisconsin, 1973), pages 43, 141, and 160.

page 103 (ornament as memory) The idea that ornament on the walls of architecture should be a revelation of earlier social and architectural history was a powerful nineteenth century concept figuring prominently in theories of Gottfried Semper and the buildings of Henri Labrouste. See David Van Zanten. "Ornament: On, In, and Through the Wall" from *Ornament, VIA III.* (Graduate School of Fine Arts, University of Pennsylvania, 1977), pages 49–50.

page 103 ("a form building force") A description coined by Jacob Schleiden from Peter Collins, *Changing Ideals in Modern Architecture* (McGill-Queens University Press, Montreal, 1965), page 151.

page 104 (synthesizing abstractions) I have taken up this subject more thoroughly in my book *Mind and Image* (University Press of Ken-

tucky, Lexington, 1976), pages 125–126.

page 105 (unconscious thought and subliminal cues) For further reading, Thomas A. Harris, *I'm OK, You're OK* (Harper and Row, New York, 1969), pages 8–12; Wilson Bryan Key, *Subliminal Seduction* (Prentice-Hall, Inc., Englewood Cliffs, N.J., 1972), and Herb Greene, *Mind and Image* (University Press of Kentucky, Lexington, 1976), pages 13–15.

page 107 (Picasso's *Man with a Sheep*) For an excellent article see Albert Elsen's "Picasso's Man with a Sheep: Beyond Good and Evil." *Art International* (March–April 1977), page 9 ff.

Chapter 8.
COLLAGE AND SURREALISM IN DESIGNING ARMATURES

page 111 (collage . . . architecture) Two recent books dealing with collage as a strategy for architecture and urban design are: Charles Jencks and Nathan Silver, *Adhocism, the Case for Improvisation* (Anchor Books, Garden City, New York, 1973); and Colin Rowe and Fred Koetter, *Collage City* (MIT Press, Cambridge, 1978).

page 117 (anti-art) For discussion of historical forces that have fostered attitudes of anti-art refer to Eric Kahler, *The Destruction of Form in the Arts* (Braziller, New York, 1968).

page 117 (Alfred North Whitehead) Passages from Whitehead are best understood in the context of his broader philosophy. Suggested are his books *The Principles of Natural Knowledge* (Cambridge University Press, 1955), and *Modes of Thought* (Capricorn Books, New York, 1958).

page 121 (Surrealism) *Architectural Design*, Volume 48, No. 2–3, (1978) was devoted to Surrealism. Two articles of particular interest are Dalibor Veseley's "Surrealism, Myth and Modernity" and Stuart Knight's "Observations on Dada and Surrealism."

page 123 (the coexistence of incompatible attitudes) E. H. Gombrich, *Art and Illusion* (Phaidon Press, London, 1977), page 96.

Index

Page numbers in *italics* refer to illustrations

127